THE ORIGIN OF FREEMASONRY AND KNIGHTS TEMPLAR

THE ORIGIN OF FREEMASONRY AND KNIGHTS TEMPLAR

COMPILED BY
JOHN R. BENNETT

Athens ‡ Manchester

The Origin of Freemasonry and Knights Templar

Published by: Old Book Publishing Ltd

The Origin of Freemasonry and Knights Templar was originally published in 1907

Copyright © 1907 John R. Bennett, P.E.C.

ISBN–10: 1-78107-003-2
ISBN–13: 978-1-78107-003-1

Cover designed by: Old Book Publishing Ltd
Book designed by: Old Book Publishing Ltd

Editor's Note

Yours fraternally

John R. Bennett

THE ORIGIN OF

Freemasonry and Knights Templar

COMPILED BY

John R. Bennett, P. E. C.

"We can not understand the actual
of a character or system without in
some degree entering into its ideal."

PRESS OF JOHNSON & HARDIN, CINCINNATI, O.

DEDICATED

TO ALL

FREEMASONS

AND

THOSE WHO LOVE THEIR

FELLOW- MEN.

CONTENTS

ILLUSTRATIONS

HISTORICAL INDEX

HISTORICAL INDEX.

HISTORICAL INDEX.

PREFACE.

In preparing this work it has been my chief aim to give to the Masonic reader a brief, concise and interesting documentary compilation of the origin of Freemasonry and Knights Templar. The authorities consulted have been those of the world's best historians and Masonic writers. In this brief history all historical facts, chronological dates, and documentary evidence have been taken from such works as Ridpath's History of the World, Joseph Francis Michaud's History of the Crusades, English and American Encyclopedias, Biblical History, Masonic Encyclopedias by Albert G. Mackey, M. D., Robert Macoy, 33°, and George Oliver, D. D., with many other works of renown, and arranged in such form as to give to the reader the greatest amount of information in the least space, saving many hours of necessary labor in the research of a large number of volumes of dry and uninteresting reading, obtaining in the end only such results as one will find within this little volume.

From my early experience in Masonic life, I learned that the character of the institution was elevated in every one's opinion just in proportion to the amount of knowledge that he had acquired of its symbolism, philosophy and history. But that few men have the time, patience or inclination to give the close and attentive reading of the greater Masonic works to acquire the knowledge that every Mason should possess.

PREFACE

In view of this fact, and a strong desire on my part to acquire more light in Masonry, I was induced some twenty years ago to commence the compilation of this concise and interesting story of Freemasonry and Knights Templar. The years of toil that I have devoted to it have been a work of love, and in placing it before the Craft, it is with the hope of the further enlightenment and betterment of mankind.

Masonry being so interwoven with the early history of the world, I have added a Supplemental Encyclopedia, in which may be found brief accounts of many ancient countries and cities, together with short sketches of the life of the early tribes and of the ancient characters connected with Masonic history.

If the reader will carefully note all references, a much better understanding of the general subjects will be had.

All Biblical chronological data will be found according to the computation of Archbishop Usher.

The illustrations in this volume are taken from Ridpath's History of the World, and are used by courtesy of the Jones Bros. Publishing Company, Cincinnati, Ohio.

JOHN R. BENNETT.

MUSKEGON, MICH., April 19, 1906.

MAP OF THE
COUNTRIES
Mentioned in the
BIBLE

FREEMASONRY.

The true history of Freemasonry is much in its character like the history of a nation. It has its historic and its prehistoric era. In its historic era, the institution can be regularly traced through various antecedent associations, similar in design and organization, to a comparatively remote period. Its connection with these associations can be rationally established by authentic documents and by other evidence which no historian would reject.

For the prehistoric era—that which connects it with the mysteries of the pagan world, and with the old priests of Eleusis, of Samothrace, or of Syria—let us honestly say that we no longer treat of Freemasonry under its present organization, which we know did not exist in those days, but of a science peculiar, and peculiar only, to the Mysteries and to Freemasonry, a science which we may call Masonic symbolism, and which constituted the very heart-blood of the ancient and the modern institutions, and gave to them, while presenting a dissimilarity of form, an identity of spirit. In connecting and tracing the germ of Freemasonry in those prehistoric days, although guided by no documents, and no authentic spoken or written narratives on which to rely, we find fossil thoughts embalmed in those ancient intellects precisely like the living ones which crop out in modern Masonry, and which, like the fossil shells and fishes of the old physical forma-

tions of the earth, show by their resemblance to living specimens the graduated connection of the past
with the present.

Every human institution is subject to great and
numerous variations; the different aspects under
which they appear, and the principles by which they
are governed, depend on the advance of civilization,
the nature of the protecting government, and the
peculiar habits and opinions of the members themselves. Before learning was advanced, and when
the art of printing was unknown, the discoveries
in the arts and sciences must of necessity have been
known to but few individuals. The pursuit of
science was a secondary matter, and questions of
philosophy were solely the prerogative of priest-
craft. Agriculture was the grand pursuit of life.
But architecture soon, in the natural order of
things, arose as a science, and human skill was
called into play. The triumph of mind over matter
was the great feat of the first architects, who were
also the first natural philosophers. There is no
speculation in the statement that these formed
themselves into an association for improvement
at an early date; their architectural monuments
preceding the authentic records of history, are with
us to this day; and tradition informs us that this
union of scientific men differed from the Freemasons of to-day in little more than in name. The
arts and sciences were cultivated in Egypt and the
adjacent countries in Asia, while all other nations
were involved in ignorance. Of these sciences,
astronomy, geometry and architecture took the
first rank.

Freemasonry not only presents the appearance

of a speculative science,[1] based on an operative art, but also very significantly exhibits itself as the *symbolic expression of a religious idea*. In other and plainer words, we see in it the important lesson of eternal life, taught by a legend which, whether true or false, is used in Masonry as a symbol and allegory. But whence came this legend? Did all lineal sources have this legend? The evidence is that they did. Not indeed the same legend; not the same personage as its hero; not the same details; but a legend with the same spirit and design; a legend funereal in character, celebrating death and resurrection, solemnized in lamentations and terminating in joy.

We can not correctly understand the history of the nations of antiquity, much less their theology, philosophy, science or ethics, without knowledge of their societies. Some of the grandest ideas, those which have had the greatest influence on human progress, were born amid mystic symbols.*

NOTE.—The asterisk (*) refers to the Supplement for further information.

Ancient Mysteries.

Among the most important of the Ancient Mysteries were the following: The Osiric in Egypt, the Adonisian in Syria, the Mithraic in Persia, the Cabiric in Thrace, the Druidical among the Celts, the Scandinavian among the Gothic, the Dionysian and Eleusinian in Greece.

Each of the Pagan gods had, beside the public, a secret worship paid him, to which none were ad-

---

[1] See Speculative Masonry in Supplement.

mitted but those who had been selected by preparatory ceremonies called *initiation*. This secret
worship was termed the MYSTERIES. And this is
supported by Strabo, who says "that it was common, both to the Greeks and the barbarians, to per-
form their religious ceremonies with the observance
of a festival, and that they were sometimes celebrated publicly and sometimes in mysterious pri-
vacy." The first of the Mysteries of which we have
any account, Warburton says, "were those of Isis
and Osiris in Egypt."

Egyptian Mysteries.

☆ Egypt has always been considered the birthplace
of the Mysteries. It was there the ceremonies of
initiation were first established. It was there that
truth was first veiled in allegory, and the dogmas
of religion were first imparted under symbolic
forms. From Egypt this system of symbols was
disseminated through Greece and Rome and other
countries of Europe and Asia, giving origin,
through many intermediate steps, to that mysterious association which is now represented by the
institution of Freemasonry. The favored rank of
the Egyptian society was the priests. To them belonged one-third of the lands of the kingdom. They
were the holy order in whose hands rested the maintenance of the national religious faith, the conduct
of all the ceremonies in the temples, the direction
of the sacrifices, the work of education and general
culture of the Egyptian. The priesthoods of Egypt
constituted a sacred caste, in whom the priestly
functions were hereditary. They exercised also

4

an important part in the government of state, and the kings of Egypt were but the first subjects of its priests.

The initiation into the Egyptian Mysteries was of all the systems practiced by the ancients the most severe and impressive. The system had been organized for ages, and the priests, who alone were the teachers of the Mysteries, were educated almost from childhood for that purpose. That "learning of the Egyptians," in which Moses is said to have been so skilled, was all imparted in those Mysteries. Over the entire history of the Land of the Pyramids a veil of mystery is drawn. Its history is a dream, not the promises of the future, but of achievements of the past. Here empire first placed her throne and swayed her scepter. Long before Greece and Rome and Assyria had been wrapped in their swaddling clothes, Egypt was a man of war and a hero of victory. The stones that reared Athens in splendor, and spoke forth the beautiful conceptions of Phidias* and Praxiteles,* were unused in the quarries long after the Colossi of Thebes had grown old with years. While Abraham, the father of the faithful, wandered a nomad and lived in tents, a Pharaoh sat on the throne of Egypt, and, but a few years after, the Ishmaelitish merchants led their camels laden with spices, balm and myrrh, commodities only used by rich and cultivated peoples, from Gilead to the Nile. A few years from this and there were standing armies in Egypt, chariots of war, bodies of infantry, and, what is still more surprising, a large body of cavalry. It was in the Egyptian society of Isis and Osiris that this ancient and wonderful civilization had its origin. Here were fashioned and wrought out those ideas that subsequently entered into the very life of the people.

The two central figures of these Mysteries, as well as of Egyptian history, were Isis and Osiris. These, when stripped of their mystic garments and brought down to the level of humanity, appear to have been an early king (Osiris) and queen (Isis) of this country, who were at the same time brother and sister. These, by superior virtue and intelligence, won the admiration and confidence of these wild and untutored barbarians, led them out of their degraded state, and guided their feet into the path of civilization and empire. Under their direction the land of savage darkness became light, and full of joy. Isis taught the people to hold the plow and turn the furrow, and to make bread from the ripened grain. While doing this she made laws for home society, and restrained men from lawlessness and violence by their sanction. Osiris built Thebes, with its hundred gates; erected temples and altars, *instituted the sacred rites,* and appointed priests to have the oversight and care of the holy things.

Having accomplished these things, and seeing their effect upon his own people, he resolved to raise a great army, and, leaving Isis as ruler, to go through all the world, "for he hoped he could civilize men and take them off from their rude and beast-like course of life." This he succeeded in doing, but shortly after his return he was slain by his brother Typhon. After his death Isis made a vow never to marry again, and spent her days in ruling justly over her subjects, "excelling all other princes in her acts of grace and bounty towards her own people, and therefore, after her death, she was num bered among the gods, and as such had divine honors and veneration, and was buried at Memphis, where they show her sepulchre at this day in the grove of Vulcan."

The sacred rites which Osiris is said to have instituted received many additions in course of time, and finally were divided into two degrees. These, as in their copy at Eleusis, Greece, were called the Great and Less, the former being the Mysteries of Osiris, the latter those of Isis, the latter being a preparation to the fuller revelation of the secrets contained in the former.

In the Great Mystery was represented the allegorical history of Osiris, which the Egyptians regarded as the most solemn mystery of their religion, and which Herodotus and all other ancient writers mention with great caution. To be initiated in these was the great privilege of the priest, though this caste were not all admitted indiscriminately to this honor. This was reserved for the heir-apparent to the throne, and for such priests as excelled in virtue and wisdom.

The principal seat of the Egyptian Mysteries was at Memphis, in the neighborhood of the great Pyramid. The legend was as follows: Osiris, a wise king of Egypt, left the care of his kingdom to his wife Isis, and traveled for three years to communicate to other nations the arts of civilization. During his absence his brother Typhon formed a secret conspiracy to destroy him and to usurp his throne. On his return Osiris was invited by Typhon to an entertainment in the month of November, at which all the conspirators were present. Typhon produced a chest inlaid with gold, and promised to give it to any person whose body would exactly fit it. Osiris was tempted to try the experiment; but he no sooner laid down in the chest than the lid was closed and nailed down and the chest thrown into the river Nile. The chest containing the body of Osiris was, after being for a long time tossed about by the waves, finally cast up at Byblos,* in Phœnicia, and left at the foot of a tamarisk* tree. Isis, overwhelmed with grief for the loss of her husband, set out on a journey, and traversed the earth in search of the body. After many adventures, she at length discovered the spot whence it had been thrown up by the waves, and returned with it in triumph to Egypt. It was then proclaimed, with the most extravagant demonstrations of joy, that Osiris was risen from the dead and had become a god. Such, with slight variations of details by different writers, are the general outlines of the Osiris legend.

It was represented in the public drama of initiation, by the image of a dead man being borne in an ark or coffin, by a procession of initiates; and this enclosure in the coffin or interment of the body was called the aphanism, or disappearance, and the lamentations for him formed the first part, or Mysteries of Isis. On the third day after the interment, the priests and initiates carried the coffin, in which was also a golden vessel, down to the river Nile. Into the vessel they poured water from the river; and then, with a cry of "We have found him, let us rejoice," they declared that the dead Osiris, who had descended into Hades, had returned from thence, and was restored again to life; and the rejoicings which ensued constituted the second part, or Mysteries of Osiris. Its resemblance to the Hiramic legend of the Masonic system will be readily seen, and its symbolism will be easily understood. Osiris and Typhon are representatives of the two antagonistic principles—good and evil, light and darkness, life and death.

Osiris as an Egyptian deity was worshiped under the form of an ox, personifying the power of good and the sunlight, united in history and in worship a sacred triad with Isis as his wife and Horus* as their child. Some of the Egyptian philosophers regarded him as a river god, and called him Nilus. But the truth is, Osiris represented the male, active or generative powers of nature; while Isis represented its female, passive or prolific powers. Thus, when Osiris was the sun, Isis was the earth, to be vivified by his rays; when he was the Nile, Isis was the land of Egypt, fertilized by his overflow.

The researches in the last few years have thrown much light on the Egyptian Mysteries. Among the ceremonies of the ancient people was one called the "Procession of Shrines," which is mentioned in the Rosetta stone,* and depicted on the temple walls. One of these shrines was an ark, which was carried in procession by the priests, who supported it on their shoulders by staves passing through metal rings. It was thus brought into the temple and deposited on a stand or altar, that the ceremonies prescribed in the ritual might be performed before it. The contents of these arks were various, but always of a mystical character. Sometimes the ark would contain symbols of life and stability, sometimes the sacred beetle, the symbol of the sun; and there was always a representation of two figures of the goddess Theme or Truth and Justice, which overshadowed the ark with their wings. These coincidences of the Egyptian and Hebrew arks must have been more than accidental.

☆ ☆

Adonisian Mysteries in Syria.

The Mysteries of Adonis, on account of their locality, bring them in close connection with the history and reputed origin of Freemasonry. They were principally celebrated at Byblos, a city in Phœnicia, situated near the base of Mount Lebanon, on the Mediterranean, north of Beyroot, and whose Scriptural or Hebrew name was Gebal, and whose inhabitants were the Giblites or Giblemites, who are referred to in the first Book of Kings (chap. v. 18) as being the "stone-squarers" employed by King Solomon in building the temple. Hence there must have evidently been a very intimate connection or frequent intercommunication between the workmen of the first temple and the inhabitants of Byblos. These Mysteries were said to have been first established at Babylon, and thence passed over into Syria, their principal seat being at Byblos, in that country.

The legend of Adonis is: That he was the King of Cyprus. Adonis was possessed of such surprising beauty that Venus* (Goddess of Love) became enamored with him, and adopted him as her favorite. Subsequently Adonis, who was a great hunter, died from a wound inflicted by a wild boar on Mount Lebanon. Venus flew to the succor of her favorite, but she came too late. Adonis was dead.

On his descent to the infernal regions Proserpine*
(Queen of Hades) became, like Venus, so attracted
by his beauty that, notwithstanding the entreaties
of the goddess of love, she refused to restore him
to earth. At length the prayers of the desponding
Venus were listened to with favor by Jupiter
(Father of Men and Gods) who reconciled the
dispute between the two goddesses, and by whose
decree Proserpine was compelled to consent that
Adonis should spend six months of each year al-
ternately with herself and Venus.

The ceremonies commenced about the season of
the year when the river Adonis began to be swollen
by the flood at its source. It is a small river of
Syria, which, rising in Mount Lebanon, enters the
Mediterranean a few miles south of Byblos. It is
a fact that, after a sudden fall of rain, the river,
descending in floods, is tinged with a deep red by
the soil of the hills in which it takes its rise, and
imparts the color to the sea, into which it is dis-
charged, for a considerable distance. The worshipers of Adonis believed that this reddish dis-
coloration of the water was a symbol of his blood.
The Israelites called him Thammuz.

The Mysteries of Adonis were celebrated
throughout all the countries of Syria,* and formed
a part of the ceremonies of the Dionysian Architects
of Tyre, by whom they were introduced into Judea.
The sacred rites began with mourning, and the days
set apart to the celebration of the death of Adonis
were passed in cries and wailing, many often
scourging themselves. On the last of the days of
mourning, funeral rites were performed in honor
of the god. On the following day the restoration

of Adonis to life was announced and was received with the most enthusiastic demonstrations of joy. The objects represented in these Mysteries were the grief of Venus and the death and resurrection of Adonis. The analogy in the symbolism that exists between Adonis in the Mysteries of the Giblemites at Byblos and Hiram the builder, can readily be seen by the Freemason in his own institution.

Dionysian Mysteries.

☆ These Mysteries were celebrated throughout Greece and Asia Minor, but principally at Athens, where the years were numbered by them. They were introduced in Greece in the year 1415 B. C. by the Egyptian colonists, many of whom, according to Biblical chronology, went there as early as 1760 B. C. These Mysteries were instituted in honor of Bacchus,* or, as the Greeks called him, Dionysus. About three hundred years afterwards, Ionic migration occurred, the emigrants carrying with them from Greece to Asia Minor the Mysteries of Dionysus, before they had been corrupted by the Athenians.

In these Mysteries the murder of Dionysus by the Titans* was commemorated, in which legend he is evidently identified with the Egyptian Osiris, who was slain by his brother Typhon.[1] The ritual of Freemasonry preserves, in its central circle, the leading features of the Dionysian institution. Hiram and Dionysus are names representing and illustrating in their history and experience the same ideas. The initiation was a symbolical prog-

[1] See page 7, last paragraph.

ress, from the dark, dead and frigid north to the refulgent east—a pilgrimage. The moral teaching of these Mysteries was the same as that of the Mysteries of Osiris.

In the time of King Solomon, the ancient city of Tyre, in Phœnicia, was celebrated as the residence of King Hiram, and to that monarch, Solomon and his father, David, were greatly indebted for assistance in the construction of the Temple at Jerusalem.

The inhabitants of Tyre were distinguished for their skill as artificers, especially as workers in brass and other metals; and it is said to have been the principal seat of that skillful body of architects known as the *Fraternity of Dionysian Architects*. The priests of Bacchus or Dionysus, having devoted themselves to architectural pursuits, founded this society, which was exclusively confined to the privilege of erecting temples and other public buildings; they were linked together by the secret ties of the Dionysian Mysteries, into which they had all been initiated. They were distinguished by many peculiarities that strikingly assimilate it to our Order. For the facilities of labor and government, they were divided into communities, each of which was governed by a Master and Wardens. They employed in their ceremonial observances many of the implements which are still to be found among Freemasons, and used, like them, a universal language, by which one brother could distinguish another in the dark as well as in the light, and served to unite the members scattered over India, Persia and Syria, into one common brotherhood. The existence of this order in Tyre, at the time of the building of the Temple of Solomon, is universally admitted; and Hiram, the widow's son, to whom Solomon intrusted the superintendence of the workmen, as an inhabitant of Tyre, was, very probably, one of its members. Hence we may legitimately suppose that the Dionysian Architects were sent by Hiram, king of Tyre, to assist King Solomon in the construction of the house he was about to dedicate to Jehovah, and that they communicated to their Jewish fellow-laborers a knowledge of the advantages of their fraternity, and invited them to a participation in its Mysteries and privileges. In the union, however, the apocryphal legend of the Dionysians would naturally give way to the true legend of the Masons, which was unhappily furnished by a melancholy incident that occurred at the time. The latter part of this statement is, it is admitted, a mere speculation, but one that has met the approval of Lowrie, Oliver and our best writers; and although this connection between the Dionysian Architects and the builders of King Solomon may not be supported by documentary evidence, the traditionary theory is at least plausible, and offers nothing that is absurd or impossible. If accepted, it supplies the necessary link which connects the Pagan* with the Jewish Mysteries.

Eleusinian Mysteries.

The institution of these Mysteries may be placed about the year 1399 B. C., in the reign of Erectheus. A fragment of marble preserved at Oxford gives this as the date. This was three hundred years prior to the reign of David in Jerusalem, and more than six hundred years before the first Olympiad,* the beginning of true Grecian history. They were celebrated at the village of Eleusis, near the city of Athens, Greece. Like the Egyptian Mysteries, they were divided into two classes, the lesser and the greater. The lesser Mysteries were celebrated on the banks of the Ilissus, whose waters supplied the means of purification of the aspirants. The greater Mysteries were celebrated in the temple at Eleusis. They were public to the many and secret to the few. They were dedicated to the goddess Demeter, the Ceres* of the Romans, who was worshiped by the Greeks as the symbol of the prolific earth; and in them were scenically represented and secretly taught the loss and recovery of Persephone, and the doctrine of the unity of God and the immortality of the soul. The scenic representations, secret signs and words of recognition, the instruction in a peculiar dogma, and the establishment of a hidden bond of fraternity, gave attraction to these Mysteries, which lasted until the very fall of the Roman Empire, and exerted a powerful influence on the mystical associations of the Middle Ages.* That which connects them with the modern initiations of Freemasonry is evident in the common thought which pervades and identifies both; though it is difficult, and perhaps impossible, to trace all the connecting links of the historic chain.

Mysteries of Mithras.

There are none of the ancient Mysteries which afford a more interesting subject of investigation to the Masonic scholar than those of the Persian god Mithras. These Mysteries are supposed to have been carried from Egypt by Zeradusht or Zoroaster, and instituted as an initiation into the principles of the religion which he had founded among the ancient Persians. Of the identity of Mithras with other deities there have been various opinions, but to the Persians, who first practiced his Mysteries, he was a sun god, and worshiped as the god of light. The Mysteries of Mithras were always celebrated in caves. They were divided into seven stages or degrees and consisted of the most rigorous proofs of fortitude and courage. The Mysteries of Mithras passed from Persia into Europe, and were introduced into Rome in the time of Pompey (87-48 B. C.). Here they flourished, with various success, until the year 378 A. D., when they were proscribed by a decree of the Senate, and the sacred cave, in which they had been celebrated, was destroyed by the Prætorian prefect. The Mithraic monuments that are still extant in the museums of Europe evidently show that the immortality of the soul was one of the doctrines taught in the Mithraic initiation.

A description of the other ancient Mysteries would only be to repeat what has been said, and as all took their rise in Egypt, we may judge the source of the fountain by the nature of the stream. All contain just such legends, everywhere differing in particulars, but everywhere coinciding in general character. After what has now been said it can not be difficult to see clearly the true end and great purpose of the Mysteries, the first and greatest fruits of which were, according to the ancients, to

civilize savage people, soften their ferocious manners, render them social, and prepare them for a
kind of life more worthy of the dignity of man.
And such were the results of the ancient legends,
taught through symbolism and mysteries.

Israelites.

Israel (Heb. Yisrael, "a prince with God"), the name bestowed upon Jacob when he wrestled with an angel at Peniel (Gen. xxxii. 28); *afterward the distinctive name of his descendants.*

MENEPTA.

Egypt. A celebrated country in the north of Africa, at the eastern part of the Mediterranean Sea. The Hebrews called it Mizrain, and hence it is now called by the Arabs, Mizr. The Greeks and Romans called it Ægyptus, whence Egypt; but the origin of this name is unknown.

Rameses the Great, of Egypt, was succeeded by King Menepta, who is now generally accepted by historians as the Pharaoh* of the exodus of Israel. The story of this remarkable race begins with the call of Abraham from his home at Ur,* the city of his birth, usually called "Ur of the Chaldees," near the Euphrates, in the northwest part of Mesopotamia,* to his promised abode in Canaan.* (See map.)

Abraham was a son of Terah, a descendant of Shem, and born in 1996 B. C. In 1922 B. C. he went to Haran,* in Mesopotamia (a region northeast of the Euphrates), accompanied by his father, his wife Sarai, his brother Nahor, and his nephew Lot* (Gen. xi. 26-32). His father dies soon after, and he takes his wife and nephew and enters the land of promise, or Canaan, as a nomad or wandering shepherd. Sojourning for a time at Shechem,* he built here, as was his custom, an altar to the Lord. Removing from place to place for convenience of water and pasturage, he was at length driven by a famine into Egypt. Returning to Canaan in 1918 B. C., rich in flocks and herds, he left Lot to dwell in the fertile valley of the lower Jordan on the plain of Sodom, and pitched his own tents in Mamre: the same is Hebron* in the land of Canaan (Gen. xii., xiii.). Here his descendants multiplied to the fifth generation. He became greatly renowned for piety and wisdom, and was called a friend of God. Sarai his wife, being barren, gives Hagar, her Egyptian handmaid, to Abram, and in 1910 B. C. Ishmael was born (Gen. xvi. 11, 12). God covenants with Abram, changes his name to Abraham, institutes circumcision, and

19

promises Isaac by Sarai, whom he calls Sarah. In fulfillment of the divine promise Isaac was born in 1896 B. C., in the extreme old age of both his parents, Abraham being 100 and Sarah ninety years of age. In 1859 B. C., Sarah dies, and five years later Abraham marries Keturah, by whom he had six sons. Abraham dies in 1821 B. C., aged 175 years. His sons Isaac and Ishmael bury him in the cave of Machpelah in the field of Ephron, which is before Mamre (or Hebron) (Gen. xxv. 9, 10).

Isaac at the age of forty marries Rebekah, his kinswoman, who bore him twin sons, Esau (or Edom) and Jacob (afterwards called Israel). They were born in 1836 B. C., but the place of their birth can not be ascertained from the narrative in Gen. xxv., except that it was in the Negeb or "South Country" of the land of Canaan. Esau was the first-born and the favorite of his father, but Jacob, in his early manhood, by the aid of his mother, obtained the birthright* (Gen. xxvii.), and in fear of the rage of Esau was sent away by his parents to his uncle Laban at Haran, in Mesopotamia, where he married his cousins Leah and Rachel, and resided twenty years, becoming wealthy in flocks and herds. Jacob then returns to Canaan with his family and his riches. Arriving near home, he meets his brother Esau, and in a rather dramatic personal interview they become reconciled (Gen. xxxiii.). Isaac dies at Hebron in 1716 B. C., aged 180 years, and is buried in the cave of Machpelah with his father. He was a man of gentle nature, a nomadic herdsman of devout and blameless life.

Joseph was the eleventh of the twelve sons of
Jacob, and was born at Haran, in Mesopotamia,
about 1745 B. C. He was the favorite son of his
father, and envied by his brethren on that account.
Their enmity was further excited by two dreams
in which his future greatness was foreshadowed,
and this led them to sell him as a slave to some
Midianite* traders, by whom he was carried into
Egypt, and sold to Potiphar, an officer of the king.
The Midianite traders were an ancient Arabian
race, the descendants of Midian, the fourth of the
six sons of Abraham by Keturah. They appear to
have dwelt mainly to the south of Moab, and covered a territory extending to the neighborhood of
Mount Sinai. Joseph acquired the confidence of
his master, who set him as overseer over all his
property, but, having repelled dishonorable propo-
sals made to him by his mistress, she accused him
falsely to her husband, and caused him to be thrown
into prison. Here he interpreted the dreams of
two of his fellow-prisoners, the chief baker and
chief butler of Pharaoh, and when his predictions
had been justified by the result, he was summoned
by King Pharaoh, at the instance of the butler, to
interpret two dreams which portended seven years
of prosperity followed by seven of famine. The
king was so much struck by the wisdom of the
advice given by the young Hebrew that he adopted
all his suggestions for making preparations for the
time of famine, and appointed him ruler over the
whole land. The measures taken by Joseph as
vizier or viceroy resulted greatly to the advantage
of the king and his people, securing an abundant
provision for the time of the famine. This calamity

extended also to the adjoining countries, and led Jacob to dispatch his sons to the Egyptian granaries to purchase corn, and there the brothers were brought face to face with Joseph, who recognized his unnatural brethren, and after a series of stratagems (Gen. xlii.), by which he reminded them of and punished them for their crime, the whole family, by his request, to the number of about seventy, was brought into and established in the "land of Goshen,"* or Ramses, as it was called by the Egyptians. (This was about 1706[1] B. C.) Here they grew and multiplied for nearly two hundred and fifteen years. Joseph married a daughter of the high priest of On (Heliopolis), and had two sons, Manasseh and Ephraim, who became the progenitors of the tribes bearing those names, the most powerful of the future kingdom of Israel. Joseph preserved his authority until his death, which occurred in 1635 B. C. at the age of 110. His body was embalmed, and at the time of the Exodus was carried to Palestine* and buried at Shechem, where his tomb is still shown.

Jacob died in Egypt in 1689 B. C., aged 147 years; his body was embalmed and buried with great pomp and all possible honors in the burial-place of Abraham, near Hebron (Gen. l.).

For a time the growing Israelitic tribe was held in honor by the government and people; but later the ruling class began to look askance at the strangers, and then to oppress them. They were set to work at building and digging. They were

---

[1] This date has been sharply contested. Some authors claim it should be about the year 1550 B. C.

set to sweat in the brickyards, and were beaten by taskmasters until they broke out in insurrection. In the course of time, denial of religious privileges complicated and intensified the rebellion. In the year 1573 B. C., Pharaoh orders all the male children of the Hebrews to be drowned. Two years later Jochebed, the wife of Amram, a Levite, succeeded in concealing her infant three months, but when she could no longer hide him, she put him in a basket of papyrus and placed the basket among the rushes of the Nile, and set his sister, Miriam, to watch from afar; finally the king's daughter found the child, and, being struck with its beauty, determined to adopt it, and sent Miriam to fetch a Hebrew nurse, who conceived the idea of getting her mother, and thus Jochebed became nurse to her own child. According to Ex. xi. 10, the child was adopted by the king's daughter, who "called his name Moses; and she said, Because I drew him out of the water." And according to Acts vii. 22, he was initiated in all the secret wisdom of the Egyptian priesthood; but the Bible tells us nothing of his youth from his adoption by the princess to the day when he slew an Egyptian overseer for his barbarous treatment of a Jewish slave. This was in the year 1531 B. C. He was then compelled to flee from Egypt, and lived many years in the land of the Midianites, with Jethro* the priest, whose daughter he married and whose flocks he tended. In 1491 B. C. he was called, according to Exodus iii., and Acts vii. 30-34, from the wilderness of Mount Sinai, where he was tending the flocks of his father-in-law, to free his brethren from slavery in which they lived. He returned to

Egypt, but at first he was received by his countrymen with suspicion, and by the Egyptians with
contempt. Nevertheless, Moses appeared as a
leader of his people, and demanded, in a personal
interview with the king at Tanis, the privilege of
conducting them a three days' march into the desert

EXODUS OF ISRAEL.

to sacrifice to Jehovah. But Pharaoh replied by
charging the Hebrews with a purpose to escape
their tasks under a pretence of piety. Whereupon
Moses, by signs and wonders done in the king's
house and kingdom, humbled the monarch and
compelled him "to let the people go" (Ex. xiii.).

After some delays the Israelites departed along

24

the banks of the canal, touching the principal Hebrew towns, and gathering their population as they went. The route then lay through the Wadi Tumilot (Valley), which extended to the Gulf of Suez, where they arrived, a few miles south of the present city of that name. Here the fugitives were hemmed in by the forces of Pharaoh, which had been sent after the retreating host. At this point in the gulf there is a shallow, stretching from shore to shore, almost fordable at low tide. "Moses stretched out his hand over the sea; and the Lord caused the sea to go back by a strong east wind all that night, and made the sea dry land, and the waters were divided." Over this the hosts of the Hebrews, numbering, it is said, 603,000 men of soldier age, or more than 2,000,000 in all, crossed to the other side in safety, which the Egyptians in pursuit essaying to do were drowned, for the waters returned to their place, while the Pharaoh's horsemen and chariots, with wheels clogged in the mire, were panic-stricken and overwhelmed.

The Israelites had no sooner escaped from the Egyptians than they were attacked at Rephidim* by the Amalekites,* whom they are said to have signally defeated (Ex. xvii.). The Amalekites were a nomadic and warlike people, of whose ancestors there is no record, but, at the time of the Exodus, they occupied the wilderness between Egypt and Palestine. They lived generally in migrating parties, in caves or in tents, like the Bedaween Arabs of the present day. After the defeat of the Amalekites, Moses led the people to Mount Sinai,* in Arabia, which is situated in that country known as the Sinaitic peninsula that lies between the horns of the Red Sea or Gulfs of Suez and Akaba, and is the place where the law of Jehovah was given and the Jewish economy instituted. The Jewish tabernacle and the ark of the covenant

HIGH PRIEST OF ISRAEL.

were here constructed in the year 1490 B. C. by Aholiab* and Bezaleel, under the immediate directions of Moses. The tribes were numbered after their families by the house of their fathers, who were the descendants of Abraham or the twelve sons of Jacob. The twelve sons were Reuben, Sim-

eon, Levi, Judah, Zebulun, Issachar, Dan, Gad,
Asher, Naphtali, Joseph and Benjamin. The
Levites were set aside to have exclusive jurisdiction
over the national worship, and as they were not to
inherit lands, the two sons of Joseph, Ephraim and
Manasseh, were chosen as their father's representatives and became progenitors in the twelve tribes
of Israel. The tribe of Levi received, instead of
a province, forty-eight cities scattered throughout
Canaan and the tenth part of the fruits of the field,
and were allowed generally to settle throughout the
land where they chose. Aaron, who was Moses'
brother, of the tribe of Levites, by a miraculous
judgment, became the first high priest. Moses directed that twelve rods should be laid up in the Holy
of Holies of the tabernacle, one for each tribe; the
name of Aaron on one rod to represent the tribe of
Levi, and Moses said, "The man's rod whom I shall
choose shall blossom." On the next day these rods
were brought out and exhibited to the people,
and while all the rest remained dry and withered,
that of Aaron alone budded and blossomed and
yielded fruit (Num. xvii.). Philo-Judæus says
that "Moses was instructed by the Egyptian
priests in the philosophy of symbols and hiero-
glyphics as well as in the mysteries of the sacred
animals." The sacred historian tells us he was
"learned in all the wisdom of the Egyptians"; and
Manetho and other traditionary writers tell us that
he was educated at Heliopolis as a priest, under his
Egyptian name of Osarsiph, and that there he was
taught the whole range of literature and science,
which it was customary to impart to the priesthood
of Egypt. It is not strange, when he began in the

wilderness to establish his new religion, that he should have given a holy use to the symbols whose meaning he had learned in his ecclesiastical education on the banks of the Nile.

The tabernacle itself was, according to Josephus, forty-five feet long by fifteen wide, its greater length being from east to west. The sides were fifteen feet

THE TABERNACLE.

high, and there was a sloping roof. There was no place of entrance except at the eastern end, which was covered by curtains. It was divided into two apartments by a richly decorated curtain. There were suspended, so as to cover the sides and top of the tabernacle, four curtains; the first or inner curtain was composed of fine linen, magnificently embroidered, with figures of cherubim, in shades of blue, purple and scarlet; this formed the "Beauti-

28

ful" ceiling. The other coverings or curtains were of goats' hair and the skins of rams and other animals colored red. The two sides and the western end were formed of boards of shittim wood, overlaid with thin plates of gold, and fixed in solid sockets or vases of silver. It was surrounded by a court, the walls of which were made of fine twined linen, attached to pillars bound with bands of silver and set in sockets of brass. The length of the court was 150 feet, its breadth 75 feet, and its height 7½ feet. The tabernacle in all its structure was arranged for convenient packing, transportation and setting up; but nevertheless, in size, in beauty of workmanship, and in costliness of material, was a magnificent structure for the wilderness. This tabernacle was carried by the Israelites in all their wanderings.

During their march through the wilderness the twelve tribes had between them four principal banners, or standards, to which reference is made in the Book of Numbers, chapter ii.: "Every man of the children of Israel shall pitch by his own standard." But as to what were the devices on the banners or what were their various colors, the Bible is absolutely silent. To the inventive genius of the Talmudists we are indebted for all that we know or profess to know on this subject. Wherever the Israelites halted they encamped with three tribes on each side of the tabernacle. The tribes of Judah, Issachar and Zebulun on the east side under the standard of Judah; Reuben, Simeon and Gad on the south side under the standard of Reuben; Ephraim, Manasseh and Benjamin on the west side under the standard of Ephraim; Dan, Asher and Naphtali on the north side under the standard of Dan; the Levites in the midst of the camp.

The Ark of the Covenant was a chest in which were kept the two tables of stone, on which were engraved the Ten Commandments. It contained likewise a golden pot of manna, Aaron's rod, and the tables of the covenant. It was always deposited in the most sacred place of the tabernacle. It was

ARK OF THE COVENANT.

made of shittim wood, overlaid within and without with pure gold. It was about three feet nine inches long, two feet three inches wide, and of the same extent in depth. It had on the side two rings of gold, through which were placed staves of shittim wood, overlaid with gold, by which, when necessary, it was borne by the Levites. Its cover or lid was of pure gold, over which were placed two figures called cherubim with expanded wings (Ex. xxv.). The cover of the ark was called Kap-

hiret, from Kaphar, "to forgive sin," and hence the
English name of "mercy-seat," as being the place
where the intercession for sin was made. Aaron's
rod was made sacred and carried in the ark from
the manner in which the tribe of Levites were chosen to be invested with the priesthood. The pot of
manna was placed in the ark of the covenant to
commemorate the heavenly bread, by which the
Israelites were sustained in the wilderness; and is
considered as a symbol of life, not the transitory,
but the enduring one of a future world.

Having again taken up their march and arriving
at the wilderness of Paran,* Moses sent twelve chosen men, one of each tribe, to examine the land of
Canaan, who, after forty days, return to Kadesh-
barnea,* a city at the southeast border of Palestine,
and bring an evil report of the land. Caleb and
Joshua, who were among those that searched the
land, said to the children of Israel, "Let us go up
at once and possess it; for we are well able to overcome it." "If the Lord delight in us, then he will
bring us into this land, and give it us, a land which
floweth with milk and honey;" but the people mur-
mur and rebel, and God swears in his wrath that
none of the murmurers shall enter the land, but be
consumed in the desert,* where they are doomed to
wander forty years. The people, however, resolve
to enter Canaan against the will of God, but
are this time repulsed by the Amalekites (Num.
xiii., xiv.). Moses then in his progress from Sinai
to Canaan, a desert march from station to station
through a period of forty years, arrives with his
people near the border of Palestine in the desert of
Zin,* and from there seeks passage through the

land of the Edomites* (descendants of Esau, Jacob's twin brother), but is positively refused and threatened with the sword should he make the attempt. Whereupon the Israelites turn away, even avoiding the Moabites* and the Ammonites* (descendants of Lot by his two daughters), but proceeded boldly against the kings of the Amorites,* Sihon, who reigned at Hesbon, and Og, at Bashan. Both of these chieftains lived east of the Jordan, and were the descendants of Canaan, an ancient patriarch, a son of Ham, and the ancestor of the Canaanites. They were dispossessed of their lands, which were bestowed on the tribes of Reuben and Gad and a half-tribe of Manasseh (Num. xxxii.). Aaron* died on Mount Hor, in Edom, Arabia,* in the fortieth year after leaving Egypt, at the age of about 123 years, and was succeeded in the priesthood by his son Eleazer. Not long after this, in the year 1451 B. C., Moses* died on Mount Nebo, one of the Abarim range of mountains, "which is in the land of Moab, that is over against Jericho," * at the age of 120, and was succeeded in authority by Joshua of the tribe of Ephraim. Joshua proved himself to be an able and resolute general. He led the tribes of Israel across the Jordan into Canaan, or the Holy Land, and then began a war of extermination upon the native inhabitants. All were exterminated except the Gibeonites,* who secured their safety by a stratagem (Josh. lx.), and became a dependent or servile class among the Hebrews.* The tabernacle was set up at Shiloh* in 1444 B. C., and the rest of the land of Palestine divided, making in all twelve confederate states according to the tribes (Josh. xviii.). Joshua died in the year 1443 B. C., at the age of 110 years. Then followed a series of judges as rulers for nearly 350 years.

In the year 1116 B. C., just before the battle of the Israelites and the Philistines* at Ebenezer, near Shiloh, the ark of the covenant was brought from Shiloh into the camp of the Israelites to inspire them with greater courage and confidence, but the Philistines overcame them, captured the ark and carried it first to Ashdod, then to Gath, and from there to Ekron. In 1115 B. C. it was returned by the Philistines from Ekron to the Israelites at Kirjath-jearim, a city of the Gibeonites situated about nine miles northwest of Jerusalem, and there placed in the house of Abinadab, a Levite, where it remained for seventy years before being conveyed to Jerusalem (I Sam. iv.-vi.).

The tabernacle was taken from Shiloh to Gibeon,* but the exact time of its removal is not known. In I. Chron. xxi. 29, it states that the tabernacle of Moses was still at Gibeon (1017 B. C.). Again, in II. Chron. i. 3-13, that the tabernacle still remained at Gibeon, and that Solomon went there to sacrifice before it. This is the last mention made of it.

Jewish History.

The first Jewish history extends from the time of the conquest of Canaan, 1445 B. C., to the establishment of the monarchy under Saul, 1095 B. C., During this period Israel was governed in the name of Jehovah by judges who were the rulers, chiefs or leaders of Israel (a theocracy). Previous to the conquest Moses had been their lawgiver and leader. After him Joshua, the general, gave the people peace by war. And after the conquest a series of rulers arose known as judges, for they

SAUL ANOINTED.

"judged Israel." Sometimes, for an interval, there was no judge at all. During such interval every man was at liberty to do what seemed good in his own eyes. By and by the example of the surrounding nations produced the infection of monarchy in

Israel. The people clamored for a king. The uncertain judgeship proved only an equivocal defense against the strong, personal governments of the adjacent pagan nations. Under the popular impulse, and against the theocratic principle, Saul, the son of Kish, of the tribe of Benjamin, was chosen for the royal honor, and was anointed king by the prophet Samuel. With this event the second period of Israelitish history begins.

Saul was a warrior. He was an austere and able man, cordially disliked by the priesthood, between whom and himself there was a conflict of authority. He began his reign by making war on the adjacent tribes, whom he reduced to subjection, the first of whom were the Ammonites. He then fell upon the Philistines, whom he routed with great slaughter in the decisive battle of Michmash. Then the Moabites, Amalekites and Edomites were successively driven beyond the borders of Israel. Meanwhile the intractable spirit of the king had given the priests opportunity to incite discontent, and an anti-Saul party had arisen among the people, and popular attention was directed to young David as the coming ruler of Israel. David was one of the most remarkable characters in history. He was a son of Jesse, and was born in Bethlehem,* Judah, about 1085 B. C. Jesse was the son of Obed and the grandchild of Boaz and Ruth. Boaz was the lineal descendant of Pharez, the son of Judah (Gen. xxxviii.; Ruth iv. 13-22).

In his youth David followed the occupation of a shepherd, and he appears to have acquired great skill as a musician. When about twenty-two years of age he was received into the household of Saul,

king of Israel, who, we are told, was troubled with
an "evil spirit." David, by playing upon the harp,
soothed and "refreshed" Saul, and the "evil spirit
departed from him." On the breaking out of war
with the Philistines in 1063 B. C. he seems to have
been released from the house of Saul, and returned
home to feed his father's sheep at Bethlehem. His
father soon after sent him to the camp of King Saul
with provisions for his brethren. On his arrival he
found the two armies drawn up in battle array,
ready for attack, and as he talked with his brethren,
Goliath, the Philistine giant, came forward, and, for
the fortieth time in as many days, offered his chal-
lenge for a single combat. David prevailed upon
Saul to let him go and meet him, whereupon he
chose five smooth stones out of the brook, and put
them in a shepherd's bag which he had, and, with
his sling in hand, he drew near to the Philistine.
Goliath came on, and "David put his hand in his
bag, and took thence a stone, and slang it, and smote
the Philistine in his forehead; and he fell upon his
face to the earth." For this and other deeds of
valor, according to the promise of the king, he received Michal, Saul's youngest daughter, in marriage. He was given a command in the army and
acquitted himself well on all occasions, and rapidly
gained the confidence and love of the people. But
Saul was offended by the praises which David received for his prowess, and not only regarded his
son-in-law with bitter jealousy, but made repeated
attempts upon his life. David at length (1056 B.
C.) was obliged to flee and seek refuge in the wilderness of Judea, where he soon gathered a band of
six hundred men, whom he kept in perfect control

and employed only against the enemies of the land. He was still pursued by Saul with implacable hostility; and, as he would not lift his hand against his king, though he often had him in his power, he at length judged it best to retire into the land of the Philistines. Here he was generously received as an enemy of Saul and of Israel, and given the town of Ziklag* as a dwelling-place, where he and his men, with their households, lived while in that country, and which has been "held by the kings of Judah unto this day."

In 1055 B. C., while the armies of the Philistines were being assembled at Aphek, a city of the tribe of Issachar, in the valley of Jezreel, preparatory to the attack upon the Israelites, who were camped at Jezreel near by in the same valley, the princes of the Philistines became suspicious of David and his forces who had accompanied them, and made complaint to Achish, their king, not to let him go into battle with them, lest he become their adversary. They said, "Is not this David of whom they sang one to another in dances, saying, Saul slew his thousand, and David his ten thousand?" Then Achish, who had become a great friend of David, sent for him, and said unto him, "Thou hast been upright, and thy going out and thy coming in with me is good in my sight, for I have not found evil in thee since the day of thy coming unto me unto this day: nevertheless the lords favor thee not. Wherefore now return, and go in peace, that thou displease not the lords of the Philistines." So David and his men returned into the land of the Philistines. On their arrival at Ziklag they found the town burned,

and their wives and their sons and their daughters
all taken captives and carried away by the Amalekites. David went at once in pursuit and soon over-
took them, where he found them scattered about,
"eating and drinking and dancing, because of all
the spoil that they had taken out of the land of the
Philistines, and out of the land of Judah." David
fought them from twilight even unto the evening of
the next day; and all that escaped were four hundred young men who rode away on camels. David
recovered all that the Amalekites had carried away
—wives, sons, daughters, and all the spoil they had
taken. On his return to Ziklag David sent a part
of the spoil unto the elders of Judah, even to his
friends, at Hebron, and to all the places where he
and his men were wont to haunt, saying, "Behold
a present for you of the spoil of the enemies of the
Lord." (In later days this would have been considered political shrewdness.)

The engagement between the Philistines and the
Israelites resulted in a complete victory for the Philistines. The Israelites fled to Mt. Gilboa, where all
the sons of King Saul were slain but one, and Saul
himself, being severely wounded, took his own life
by falling upon his sword. The death of Saul
opened the way for David to the promised throne.
He was at once chosen king over the tribe of Judah,
reigning at Hebron for seven years, while Ishbosheth, Saul's only remaining son, was recognized as
king of Israel, and in power on the east side of the
Jordan, and for two years was obeyed by all the
tribes except Judah. In 1048 B. C., Ishbosheth was
assassinated, and David became king over *all Israel*
(I. Sam. xvi.; II. Sam. i.-v.)

One of the first acts of his reign was the conquest of Jerusalem, the principal town of the Jebusites, who were descendants of Canaan and occupied that part of the land of Canaan (Palestine) situated south of the center of the country, about thirty-seven miles from the Mediterranean, and about twenty-four miles from the river Jordan; an elevated ground upon which rests the city of Jerusalem, which they called Jebus. The old traditions and natural prepossessions both of Jews and Christians connect it with Salem, of which Melchizedek was king (Gen. xlv.). The Jebusites seem to have been territorially one of the smallest of the Canaanitish nations, but from their position one of the strongest.

In the conquest of Canaan, their king, Adoni-Zedek, was slain by Joshua at Makkedah, after the battle of Beth-horon (Josh. x.). After Joshua's death (1443 B. C.) the Israelites obtained possession of the town, which they afterwards jointly inhabited with the Jebusites for nearly 400 years. When David became king (1055 B. C.) he expelled the latter and made it the capital of his kingdom, under the name of Jebus-salem or Jerusalem, where he reigned for thirty-three years. In 1045 B. C. the ark of the covenant, which was at Kirjath-jearim, was carried, under King David's instructions, to Jerusalem, where it was placed in a temporary tabernacle erected for its use. Here the priests performed their daily service until Solomon erected the temple, then the temporary or Davidic tabernacle was put away as a relic. Both the old, or Sinaitic, and Davidic tabernacles were in time altogether lost sight of, and no doubt became victims of carelessness and the corroding influence of time or were burned up. David died in 1015 B. C., having reigned forty years, and was by far the greatest monarch that ever sat on the throne of Israel. Solomon, who succeeded to the throne, was the son of David by Bathsheba, whose husband, Uriah, he caused to be basely slain (II. Sam. xi., xii.).

King Solomon's Temple.

It was King David who first proposed to substitute for the nomadic tabernacle a permanent place of worship for his people. For this purpose he purchased Mount Moriah, one of the eminences of the ridge which was known as Mount Zion, and was the property of Ornan, the Jebusite, who used it as a threshing-floor. But, although King David had designed the temple and acquired all the necessary means, and even collected many of the materials, he was not permitted to commence the undertaking, and the execution of the task was left to his son and successor, Solomon. Accordingly that monarch laid the foundation of the edifice in the fourth year of his reign, 1012 B. C., and with the assistance of his friend and ally, Hiram, king of Tyre, completed it in about seven years and a half, dedicating it to the service of the Most High in the year 1004 B. C. This was the year of the world 3000, according to the Hebrew chronology; and although there has been much difference among the chronologists in relation to the precise date, this is the one that has been generally accepted, and it is therefore adopted by Masons in their calculations of different epochs.

☆ When Solomon was about to build the Temple (II. Chron. i. 10) he called upon Hiram, king

THE TEMPLE OF SOLOMON.

of Tyre, to furnish him with a supply of timber. The Tyrian king not only supplied him with the timber, which was cut in the forest of Lebanon by the Sideonites and sent on floats by sea to Joppa,* a distance of over one hundred miles, and thence carried by land about forty miles to Jerusalem, but also sent him a man by the name of Hiram Abiff, the most accomplished designer and operator then known in the country. Tyre* and Sidon* were the chief cities of the Phœ-

41

nicians.[1] Tyre was distant from Jerusalem about one hundred and twenty miles by sea, and was thirty miles nearer by land. Sidon was under the Tyrian Government, situated twenty miles north of Tyre in the forests of Lebanon. It was a place of considerable importance even in the time of Joshua (1451 B. C.), who succeeded Moses, and who spoke of it as "Great Sidon." Hence it is evident that the Phœnicians were *far advanced in the arts of life* when the Israelites reached the promised land. That no confusion might arise, owing to the great numbers employed, King Solomon selected those of most enlightened minds, religious and zealous in good work, as masters to superintend the workmen; and for overseers of the work he selected men who were skillful in geometry and proportion, and who had been initiated and proved in the mystical learning of the ancient sages. He numbered and classed all the craftsmen, whether natives or foreigners. At the completion of the temple, the ark of the covenant was deposited by Solomon in the Sanctum Sanctorum, or Holy of Holies, of the temple. It was lost upon the final destruction of the building by the Chaldeans in 588 B. C. The first temple of the Jews was called the palace or the house of Jehovah to indicate its splendor and magnificence, and was intended to be the perpetual dwelling-place of the Lord. It was one of the most magnificent structures of the ancient world. It was surrounded with spacious courts, and the whole structure occupied at least half a mile in circumference. This was surrounded by a wall of great height, exceeding in

---

[1] See Phœnicians, in Supplement.

44

the lowest part four hundred and fifty feet, constructed entirely of white marble. The body of the temple was in size much less than many a modern parish church, for its length was but ninety feet,[1] or, including the porch, one hundred and five, and its width but thirty, being just twice the size of the old or Sinaitic tabernacle. It was its outer courts, its numerous terraces, and the magnificence of its external and internal decorations, together with its elevated position above the surrounding dwellings, which produced that splendor of appearance that attracted the admiration of all who beheld it and gave cause for the queen of Sheba,* when it first broke upon her view, to exclaim in admiration, "A Most Excellent Master must have done this!"

The twelve tribes of Israel were all engaged in its construction, and for its erection David had collected more than four thousand millions of dollars, and 184,600 men were engaged about seven and one-half years in building it; after its completion it was dedicated by Solomon with solemn prayer, and seven days of fasting, during which a peace-offering of twenty thousand oxen and six times that number of sheep was made, to consume which the holy fire came down from heaven.

The Exploration of Jerusalem.

Recent explorations of Jerusalem by an association known as "The Palestine Exploration Fund" of

---

[1] Temple measurements are based upon a cubit of eighteen inches.

England, with Captain Charles Warren in charge, have made many discoveries that go to corroborate the testimony of Josephus and of Scriptural writers of the earlier history of the Holy City.

The present city of Jerusalem stands, as it were, *upon a heap of dust and rubbish,* under which is the Jerusalem of the Bible. The fact that ancient Jerusalem was seventeen times captured, and more than once leveled to the ground, its splendid edifices converted into piles of dust and ruins, is not sufficient altogether to account for this singular situation, but it is rather to the fact that the stone of which the houses and walks of Jerusalem are built is very friable and exfoliates rapidly, so rapidly that a few centuries are sufficient to reduce a square block to a shapeless mass. This, of course, produces pulverized earth, the earth which has buried fifty, seventy-five and even a hundred feet deep, the Jerusalem of our Saviour's period. The so-called "Jerusalem marble," taken from the immense quarry which underlies so much of the northeastern quarter of the city, and which has been excavated during the last three thousand years expressly for building materials, is so soft when it first comes from the quarry that it may almost be crushed between the fingers. It is but little firmer than a well-crystallized loaf of sugar. True, it hardens upon exposure, and in time becomes a fair material for building purposes; but if any one is surprised to find the city of Jerusalem standing upon a pile of disintegrated limestone, fifty feet thick, as it surely does, he has only to explore that enormous quarry, a quarter of a mile deep, to discover where the rubbish originally came from.

This explanation will enable the reader to understand what is meant by *exploring Jerusalem*. It is simply to go to the bottom of that enormous mound of dust and ashes, and let in the light upon streets and foundations upon which it shone two thousand years ago. In this respect there is a most exact analogy between the exploration of Jerusalem and of Pompeii. Over the latter city the superincumbent mass is scoriae, lava and volcanic ashes; in the former the accumulations are of pulverized limestone, added, of course, to the garbage of the city, shreds of pottery, bones, etc., etc., the accumulations of that extended period. It is no romance to say that the present Jerusalem overlies *many Jerusalems* that have gone to dust, in the centuries since the Jebusites established their citadel upon Mount Zion, before the time of Abraham, and that the explorer's spade must pass these graves of cities one by one to find the remnants which he seeks. These remarks are likewise applicable to the old sites of Tyre, Sidon, Gebal, etc.

The Foundation of the Temple.

It is difficult for the superficial reader to comprehend that although the temple of Solomon is *absolutely gone*—effaced from the earth, so that not a crumb or fragment can be recognized—yet its foundation remains. By this term is not meant the *walls* upon which the temple was built (comparing it with an ordinary edifice), but the *platform*, the hill, the mound artificially erected to serve as a basis for the sublime structure.

The hill, styled in the Old Testament Moriah,

and more recently *Mount* Moriah, was, by nature, a narrow, knobby, crooked ridge (of the class familiarly known as "hog back"), deeply channeled by ravines and gulleys, honeycombed with caves, and in no proper sense fit to be used as the basis of a great temple. On all sides it fell off rapidly and very steeply, except from northwest to southeast, the direction in which the ridge ran. The area on the summit was enlarged by walls built along the declivities, the outside wall deep down the valleys, from 100 to 150 feet below the area on which the temple buildings stood. One hundred feet again below this lay the original bed of the brook Kedron. The foundations of the temple, therefore, were 250 feet above the deep defiles around. This area, originally built by Solomon and enlarged by Herod, still exists, running on the south along the valley of Hinnom 1,000 feet and along the Kedron 1,500. To transform this unsightly and circumscribed ridge into a solid, broad, high and durable platform was a problem of stupendous magnitude— as great a one, perhaps even greater, than would have been that of making a platform entirely artificial.

To illustrate and convey a partial idea of the task that devolved upon Hiram and his builders: Go out upon a level plain; measure off an oblong square, 1,600 feet by 1,000, equal to thirty-six and a half acres; build a wall around it of great stones, eight, ten, twenty, and even forty feet long, and of proportionate breadth and thickness; bind the foundation-stones of this wall firmly together with clamps of iron and lead, and in the same manner fasten them into the native rock that lies below; raise that wall to an average height of one hundred and fifty feet of solid masonwork; *fill up* solid the whole area of thirty-six and a half acres to that great height of one hundred and fifty feet! This being done, you will have such a platform as was erected by Solomon's craftsmen, upon which to build the temple.

The figure is not absolutely. correct, for there was a central core to the platform, viz.: the original Mount Moriah, and in the masonwork many large vaults and subterranean chambers were left.

Now, when we describe the foundations of King Solomon's temple as still remaining, we allude to this stupendous base, the platform of thirty-six and a half acres, constructed in so substantial a manner that neither time, nor the devastation of barbarian force, nor the mighty bruit of earthquakes, has had power to break it up. So large are the stones of which the outer walls are built, so artistically are they laid together in relation to each other, and so firmly morticed at their interior edges and at their points of junction with the native rock, that it is safe to say that no power that human hands can apply will ever remove them, nor will any volcanic force affect them, less than that which would elevate the bed of the sea and sink the mountains into the depths.

On top of and along the outer walls of this inclosure or foundation were built the porticoes or covered walks, above which were galleries or apartments, supported by pillars of white marble, that overlooked the brook Kedron and the valley of Hinnom. They were magnificent structures, resembling the nave and aisles of Gothic cathedrals. But these were only the outer buildings of the temple area. The porticoes opened inwardly upon a court paved

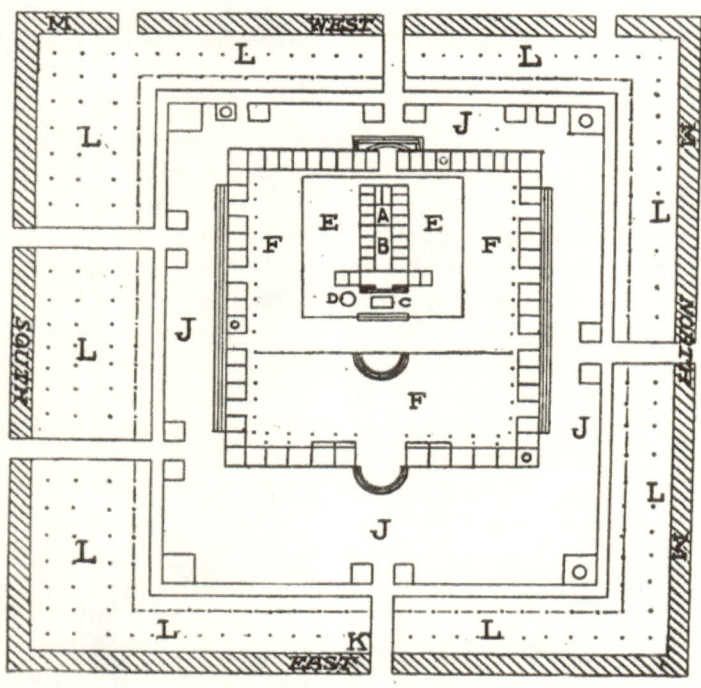

PLAN OF TEMPLE.

A. The Holy of Holies.
B. The Holy Place.
C. The Altar of Burnt Offerings.
D. The Brazen Laver.
E. The Court of the Priests.
F. The Court of Israel.
J. The Court of the Gentiles.
K. The Eastern Gate.
L. Porches or Colonnades.
M. Outer Wall.

with marble and open to the sky. This was called the "Court of the Gentiles," because the Gentiles were admitted into it, but were prohibited from passing farther. It was the exterior court, and by far the largest of all the courts belonging to the temple. It entirely surrounded the other courts and the temple itself.

Passing through the court of the Gentiles, you enter the Court of Israel, which was divided by a low stone wall into two divisions, the outer one being occupied by the women, from which an ascent is made of fifteen steps to the inner one, which was occupied by the men. In this court, and the piazza which surrounded it, the Israelites stood in solemn and reverent silence while their sacrifices were burning in the inner court, or "Court of the Priests," and while the services of the sanctuary were performed.

The "Court of the Priests" was within the Court of Israel and surrounded by it. Within this court stood the brazen altar on which the sacrifices were consumed, the molten sea in which the priests washed, and the ten brazen lavers for washing the sacrifices; also the various utensils and instruments used for sacrificing. To this court the people brought their oblations and sacrifices, but none were permitted to enter but the priests who prepared and offered the sacrifice. From the Court of the Priests twelve steps ascended to the temple, strictly so called, which was divided into three parts, the porch, the sanctuary and the Holy of Holies. At the entrance to the porch of the temple was a gate made entirely of brass, the most precious metal known to the ancients. Beside this gate and just under the porch there were two pillars, Jachin and Boaz. These pillars were twenty-seven feet high and six feet through. The thickness of the brass of each pillar was three inches. The one that stood on the right hand (or south) was called Jachin, and the other at the left hand (or north) was called Boaz. It has been supposed that Solomon, in erecting these pillars, had reference to the pillar of cloud and pillar of fire, which went before the Israelites in their journey through the wilderness, and that the right-hand or south pillar represented the pillar of cloud and the left-hand or north pillar represented that of fire. Solomon did not simply erect them as ornaments to the temple, but as memorials of God's repeated promises of support to his people of Israel. For the pillar (Jachin), derived from the Hebrew words (Jah), "Jehovah," and (achin), "to establish," signifies that "God will establish his house of Israel"; while the pillar (Boaz), compounded of (b), "in," and (oaz), "strength," signifies that "in strength shall it be established." And thus were the Jews, in passing through the porch to the temple, daily reminded of the abundant promises of God, and inspired with confidence in his protection and gratitude for his many acts of kindness to his chosen people. If this symbolism be correct, the pillars of the porch, like those of the wilderness, would refer to the superintending and protecting power of Deity. (Calcott, Cand. Disg., 66.)

From the porch you enter the sanctuary by a portal, which, instead of folding-doors, was furnished with a magnificent veil of many colors, which mystically represented the universe. In the sanctuary were placed the various utensils necessary for the daily worship. The Holy of Holies, or innermost chamber, was separated from the sanctuary by doors of olive, richly sculptured and inlaid with gold and covered with veils of blue, purple, scarlet, and the finest linen. Into the most sacred place the high priest alone could enter, and that only once a year, on the day of atonement.

If one looked upon Mount Moriah from the brow of Mount Olivet opposite, and beheld the city from the direction of Bethany, it must have been a sight which, for architectural beauty and grandeur, perhaps, has never been equaled, certainly not surpassed. It was an artificial mountain from the deep ravines below, wall, column, roof, pinnacle, culminating in the temple within and above all, and probably measuring between 500 and 600 feet in height.

James Fergusson, Esq., the distinguished architect, writes: "The triple temple of Jerusalem, the lower court standing on its magnificent terraces, the inner court raised on its platform in the center, and the temple itself rising out of the group and crowning the whole, must have formed, when combined with the beauty of the situation, one of the most splendid architectural combinations of the ancient world."

Josephus wrote: "If any one looked down from the top of the battlements he would be giddy, while his sight could not reach to such an immense depth." This passed for foolish exaggeration till recent explorations vindicated the statement.

Croley (in Salathiel), in his magnificent word-painting, describes the mountain and its glorious occupant (Temple of Herod [1]), the year of its destruction, A. D. 70, which was similar in structure to the Temple of Solomon, as follows: "I see

---

[1] See Temple of Solomon, in Supplement.

the Court of the Gentiles circling the whole, a fortress of the purest marble, with its wall rising six hundred feet from the valley; its kingly entrance, worthy of the fame of Solomon; its innumerable and stately buildings for the priests and officers of the temple, and above them, glittering like a succession of diadems, those alabaster porticoes and colonnades in which the chiefs and sages of Jerusalem sat teaching the people, or walked, breathing the air, and gazing on the grandeur of a landscape which swept the whole amphitheater of the mountains. I see, rising above this stupendous boundary, the court of the Jewish women, separated by its porphyry pillars and richly sculptured wall; above this the separated court of the men: still higher, the court of the priests; and highest, the crowning splendor of all the central temple, the place of the sanctuary, and of the Holy of Holies, covered with plates of gold, its roof planted with lofty spearheads of gold, the most precious marbles and metals everywhere flashing back the day, till Mount Moriah stood forth to the eye of the stranger approaching Jerusalem, what it had been so often described by its bards and people, *a mountain of snow studded with jewels.*"

All these buildings, porticoes, columns, pinnacles, altar and temple, have perished. "Not one stone remains upon another which has not been thrown down." The area alone remains, and the massive substructures for 3,000 years have been sleeping in their courses. The preservation has been due to the ruin. Buildings so vast have been toppled down the slopes of the Moriah, that the original defiles and valleys have been almost obliterated.

What has been regarded as the original surface has been found to be debris from 70 to 90 feet deep.

With pickaxe and shovel British explorers have been down to the original foundations. Fallen columns have been met with and avoided, or a way blasted through them. The cinders of burnt Jerusalem have been cut through and turned up to the light—rich moulds deposited by the treasures of Jewish pride. The seal of Haggai, in ancient Hebrew characters, was picked up out of the siftings of this deposit. The first courses of stones deposited by Phœnician builders have been reached, lying on the living rock. Quarry-marks, put on in vermilion, have been copied—known to be quarry-marks by the trickling drops of paint, still visible—only they are above the letters, showing that when they were written the stones lay with the underside uppermost.

The whole of Mount Moriah has been found to be fairly honeycombed with cisterns and passages. One of the cisterns, known as the Great Sea, would contain two millions of gallons, and all together not less than ten millions. The wall of Ophel has been exposed—at the present time 70 feet high—though buried in debris; and the remains of towers and houses have been lighted upon belonging to the age of the kings of Judah.

The seven successive objects that have occupied this sacred ridge, to which a Mason's attention is directed, are:

1. The Altar of Abraham.
2. The Threshing-floor of Ornan.
3. The Altar of David.
4. The Temple of Solomon.

5. The Temple of Zerubbabel.
6. The Temple of Herod.
7. The Mosque of Omar. In the fourtenth century this building was described as a very fair house, lofty and circular, covered with lead, well paved with white marble.

The temple area is now occupied by two Turkish mosques, into which, until recently, neither Jew nor Christian was permitted to enter.

Ancient Temples.

The Egyptian form of a temple was borrowed by the Jews, and with some modifications adopted by the Greeks and Romans, whence it passed over into modern Europe.

The direction of an Egyptian temple was usually from east to west, the entrance being at the east. It was a quadrangular building, much longer than its width, and was situated in the western part of a sacred enclosure. The approach through this enclosure to the temple proper was frequently by a double row of Sphinxes. In front of the entrance were a pair of tall obelisks, which will remind the reader of the two pillars at the porch of Solomon's temple. The temple was divided into a spacious hall, where the great body of the worshipers assembled. Beyond it, in the western extremity, was the cell or sekos, equivalent to the Jewish Holy of Holies, into which the priests only entered; and in the remotest part, behind a curtain, appeared the image of the god seated on his shrine or the sacred animal which represented him.

The Grecian temples like the Egyptian and the

Hebrew, were placed within an inclosure, which was separated from the profane land around it, in early times, by ropes, but afterwards by a wall. The temple was usually quadrangular, although some were circular in form. It was divided into parts similar to the Egyptian.

The Roman temples, after they emerged from their primitive simplicity, were constructed much upon the mode of the Grecian. The idea of a separation into a holy and a most holy place has everywhere been preserved. The same idea is maintained in the construction of Masonic Lodges, which are but imitations, in spirit, of the ancient temples. The Most Holy Place of the Egyptians and Jews was in the West, whereas now it is in the East.

Division of the Hebrew Nation.

Solomon died in the year 975 B. C. During his reign he peacefully consolidated and recaptured, fortified or built cities or stations for commerce or protection at strategic points. He built reservoirs, aqueducts, many wonderful buildings, and laid out "paradises" and gardens. Many kings were his tributaries; untold wealth and the wonders and curiosities of many countries flowed into or through the land, so that "silver was nothing accounted of in his day." Many foreigners were attracted by his splendor and wisdom, notably Balkis (?), the queen of Sheba, with her marvelous retinue. To meet with Oriental ideas of his royal magnificence, his harem grew to number one thousand inmates, and, contrary to the law of Moses, he not only multiplied wives, but by his marriages formed alliances with many heathen nations. In his old age his "strange" wives led him to commit or permit gross and vicious idolatry. He was gifted with transcendent wisdom and the most brilliant mental powers, yet towards the end of his life he presented the sad spectacle of a common eastern despot, voluptuous, idolatrous, occasionally even cruel, and his reign can not but be regarded, both politically and financially, as a splendid failure. Before his death Edom and Syria revolted, tribal jealousies arose in Israel, and Jeroboam, of the tribe of Ephraim, who was superintendent of the public works, began to plot the division of the nation, in which he was aided by the alienation of the people coming through the intolerable oppression and taxation that were necessary to meet the enormous expenses of the court. For this conspiracy Jeroboam was forced to flee to save his life. He went to Egypt and placed himself under the protection of Shishak, the king.

Hardly had Solomon breathed his last when his people arose in revolt. Rehoboam, his son and successor, whose mother was Naamah, an Ammonite, adopted his father's methods as his own, and with a haughty air unwisely provoked the resentment which justice and policy called upon him to allay. Ten tribes, under the leadership of Jeroboam, who, after the death of Solomon, had returned to Jerusalem, seceded from his dominion and formed the nation or kingdom of Israel, and took up their residence in Samaria; while the remaining two, the tribes of Judah and Benjamin, retained possession of the Temple and of Jerusalem under the name of the Kingdom of Judah.* Thus, in 975 B. C., was effected the division of the Hebrew nation into peoples who ever afterwards maintained towards each other an attitude of estrangement and hostility. In the following year Jeroboam, king of Israel, abolished the worship of Jehovah and established that of the golden calves at Dan and Bethel. The priests and Levites and pious Israelites leave their possessions in the kingdom of Israel and are incorporated in the kingdom of Judah.

The Temple retained its splendor only thirty-three years, for in the year 971 B. C., Shishak, the king of Egypt, made war upon the king of Judah, took Jerusalem and carried away the choicest treasures. From that time to the period of its final destruction the history of the Temple is but a history of alternate spoliations and repairs, of profanations and idolatry and subsequent restorations to a purity of worship.

☆ After the completion of the Temple, having finished that great work, and filled all Judea with temples and palaces and walled cities (II. Chron. xi.; I. Kings ix.), having enriched and beautified Gezer, Baalah and Tadmor with the results of their genius, many of these "cunning workmen," or members of the Fraternity of Architects, passed into Greece, Rome, Spain, and other countries, wherever their services could be employed in the erection of famous edifices for which the ancient world is justly celebrated.

About the year 721 B. C. the army of Shalmaneser IV., king of Assyria, invaded Samaria, the home of the descendants of the ten revolted tribes, captured the city of Samaria, the capital, and caused the downfall of the kingdom of Israel. Hoshea, its sovereign, was thrown into prison, the greater part of the inhabitants carried away captive into the far East, the mountainous regions of Media, and their place supplied by Assyrian colonists brought from Babylon, Persia, Shushan, Elam, and other places. These colonists brought with them the idolatrous creed and practices of the region from which they emigrated. They mingled with the remnant of the Israelites, intermarried and formed the mixed people called Samaritans.* The Israelites who had been exiled never returned, and what became of them has always been, and we presume will always remain, matter of vaguest speculation.

Ancient to Modern.

In passing from this brief outline of the condition of the fraternity in what we may properly denominate the ancient history, we will now endeavor to trace its progress from that period to the more enlightened days of modern architecture, and the cultivation of the arts and sciences, in such chronological order as will give the most concise historical facts, based upon substantial documents, and the principal monuments erected by the traveling operative fraternities or Freemasons.

Roman Colleges of Artificers.

☆ In 716 before the Christian era, the *Roman colleges of Artificers* were established. They were composed of men learned in all the arts and trades necessary for the execution of civil, religious, naval and hydraulic architecture, with their own laws and judges, laws based on those of the Dionysian Artificers,[1] whose mysteries had spread among the principal peoples of the East. (See Dionysian Mysteries, p. 12). Numa, the great lawgiver, the second king of Rome, in founding these colleges, made them at the same time civil and religious societies, with the *exclusive* privilege of building temples and edifices, their relations to the state and priesthood being determined by the general laws. At their head were presidents called Masters, Overseers or

---

[1] "The papal briefs which protected them alleged that immunities were given them, after the example of Hiram, king of Tyre, when he sent artisans to King Solomon, for the purpose of building the temple at Jerusalem" (Royal Masonic Cyclopedia, p. 741).

Wardens, Censors, Treasurers, Keepers of the Seals, Architects and Secretaries; there was in each of them a priest. The Workmen were divided into three classes: Elders, or chief men of the trade, and their journeymen and apprentices; they had secret meetings; paid monthly dues, by which means a common fund was accumulated for the maintenance or relief of indigent or destitute members; they elected the candidates for admission by voice of the members, and performed a secret ceremony of initiation and made a symbolic use of the implements of their art or profession. No college could consist of less than three members. In all these respects they were like modern Lodges of Freemasonry. With the advance of the empire, their numbers increased and their privileges greatly extended, so that they became an important element in the body politic.

The Romans were early distinguished for a spirit of colonization, which was conducted through the legionary soldiers of the army. To each legion there was attached a College or Corporation of Artificers, which was organized with the legion at Rome, and passed with it through all its campaigns, and when it colonized remained in the colony to plant the seeds of Roman civilization, and to teach the principles of Roman arts. The members of the college erected fortifications for the legions in times of war, and in times of peace, or when the legion became stationary, constructed temples and dwelling-houses. When England was invaded by the Roman armies in the year 55 B. C., the legions which went there carried with them their Colleges of Artificers. One of these legions, under Julius

Cæsar, advancing into the northern limits of the country, established a colony, and, to defend themselves, formed an entrenched camp with walls, inside of which, as elsewhere, habitations, temples and aqueducts appeared, which, under the name of Eboricum, gave birth to the city of York, afterwards so celebrated in the history of Masonry. In the beginning of the second century, after the fall of the Roman Republic, all the Colleges of Artificers lost their ancient privileges. But in the year 286, Carausius, known as the "Count of the Saxon Shore," and "Admiral of the Northern Seas," was besought by the Britons,* suffering from the depredations of the Saxon and Frank pirates, to assume the sovereignty of their island. Having organized a marine victorious against the pirates, which before his advent had filled the "narrow seas," he took possession of Britain and declared himself emperor. In order to conciliate the Roman Colleges of Artificers, then wielding an immense influence in that country, he restored their ancient privileges, since which time they have been called *privileged* or *Freemasons*, to distinguish them from those not thus entitled. In 294 Carausius was assassinated by his prime minister and confidential friend, Allectus, who maintained his usurped dominions for three years, when Roman power put an end to the independent sovereignty of Britain, and reunited it with the empire.

The invasion of the northern barbarians into Italy demanded the entire force of the Roman armies to defend the integrity of the empire at home. Britain in the year 420 was abandoned, and the natives, principally Celts, with the

Roman colonists, and the Colleges of Artificers, who had settled among them, were left to defend themselves. Long previous to this, however, Christianity had dawned, not only upon the British Islands, but upon the whole of Europe, and the influences of the new faith were not long in being felt by the colleges, and the next phase in their history is the record of their assumption of the Christian life and doctrines.

☆ ☆

Building Corporations.

☆ As soon as the colonists and the natives of Britain had been abandoned, they were driven, first by the Picts, their savage neighbors, and then by the Saxon sea robbers, into the mountains of Wales and the islands of the Irish Sea. The Artificers, who were converted to Christianity, and who had remained when the legions left the country, went with them, and having lost their connection with the mother institution at Rome, became thenceforth simply *Building Corporations* or *Societies of Builders*. They retained the organization which had always worked so well and the name of Freemasons. Subsequently, in the sixth century, about the year 550, when the whole of England was taken possession of by the Saxon invaders, the Britons, headed by the monks and priests, and accompanied by the Artificers, fled into Ireland and Scotland which countries they civilized and converted, and whose inhabitants were instructed in the art of building.

Whenever we read of the extension in barbarous

or pagan countries of Christianity, and the conversion of their inhabitants to the true faith, we also hear of the propagation of the art of building in the same places by the corporations of architects, the immediate successors of the Roman legionary colleges, for the new religion required churches, and, in time, cathedrals and monasteries, and the ecclesiastical architecture speedily suggested improvements in the civil. In time, all the religious knowledge and all the architectural skill of the northern part of Europe were concentrated in the remote regions of Ireland and Scotland, whence missionaries were sent back to England to convert the pagan Saxon. From England these energetic missionaries, accompanied by the pious Architects, passed into Europe, and effectually labored for the conversion of the Scandinavian nations, introducing into Germany, Sweden, Norway, and even Ireland, the blessings of Christianity, and the refinements of civilized life.

The religious contest between the original Christians of Britain and the Papal power, after years of controversy, finally terminated in the submission of the British bishops to the Pope. As soon as the Papal authority was firmly established over Europe, the Roman Catholic hierarchy secured the services of the builders' corporations, and these, under the patronage of the Pope and the bishops, were everywhere engaged as "Traveling Freemasons," in the construction of ecclesiastical and regal edifices. Henceforth we find these corporations of builders exercising their art in all countries, everywhere proving by the identity of their designs that they were controlled by universally accepted principles, and showing in every other way the characteristics of a corporation or guild.

In England the Fraternities of Builders or Freemasons were subject to many adverse difficulties, from the repeated invasions of Scots, Picts, Danes and Saxons, which impeded their active labors, yet were they enabled to maintain their existence according to the oldest manuscript extant, until in the year 926, they held that General Assembly at the city of York which framed the constitutions that governed the English Craft for eight hundred years. In that manuscript was found the following legend, which Freemasonry of the present day accepts as genuine portions of authentic history. The legend was given by Dr. Anderson in the first Book of Constitutions in 1723, and afterwards accepted and published by William Preston in the following words: "Edward (the Elder) died in 924 and was succeeded by Athelstane,* his son, who appointed his brother, Edwin, patron of the Masons. This prince procured a charter from Athelstane, empowering them to meet annually in communication at York. In this city the first Grand Lodge of England was formed in 926, at which Edwin presided as Grand Master. Here many old writings were produced in Greek, Latin and other languages, from which it is said the Constitutions of the English Lodge have been extracted." It is that code of laws adopted at that General Assembly in 926, which became the basis on which all subsequent Masonic Constitutions were framed. (See York, in Supplement.)

The calling of this Assembly proves that the Freemasons were previously in activity in the kingdom, which is, in fact, otherwise proved by records of the building by them, at an earlier period, of cathedrals, abbeys and castles. But we date the York Assembly as the first known and acknowledged organization of the Craft in England into a national body or Grand Lodge.

After that General Assembly, the fraternity experienced, as in other countries, its alternate periods of prosperity and decay. For a long time the York Assembly exercised the Masonic jurisdiction over all England; but in 1567 the Masons of the southern part of the island elected Sir Thomas Gresham, the celebrated merchant, their Grand Master. He was succeeded in turn by Chas. Howard, Earl of Effingham, and George Hastings, Earl of Huntingdon, and they in 1607 by the illustrious architect, Inigo Jones,* who inspired great spirit into the Lodges. Men, not architects nor masons, but eminent for learning, knowledge or position, were admitted as members of the body under the designation of *Accepted* brethren; hence the origin of the present style of the society, FREE AND ACCEPTED MASONS.

Speculative Masonry.

☆ There were now two Grand Masters in England who assumed distinctive titles; the Grand Master of the North being called "Grand Master of All England," while he who presided in the South was called "Grand Master of England." In the beginning of the eighteenth century Masonry in the south of England had fallen into decay. The disturb-

ances of the revolution, which placed William III.
on the throne (1689), and the subsequent warmth
of political feelings, gave the Order a wound fatal
to its success. Sir Christopher Wren,* long active
as a Master-builder and Grand Master in the reign
of Queen Anne (1702-1714), the last of his royal
patrons, had become aged, infirm and inactive,
and hence the general assemblies of the Grand
Lodge had ceased to take place. In 1715 there were
but four Lodges in the south of England and all
working in the city of London. These Lodges,
being desirous of reviving the prosperity of the
Order, determined to unite themselves under a new
Grand Master, and revive the communications and
annual festivals of the society. They therefore
"met at the Apple-tree Tavern" and constituted
themselves a Grand Lodge, *pro tempore,* in due
form. They resolved to hold the annual assembly
and feast, and then to choose a Grand Master from
among themselves. Accordingly on St. John the
Baptist's day (June 24) in 1717, the annual assembly and feast were held and Mr. Anthony Sayer·
was duly proposed and elected Grand Master. A
statute was enacted which entirely changed the
objects of the institution. From an operative society it became wholly speculative in its character.
It ceased to build material temples, and devoted
itself to the erection of a spiritual one. It retained
the working tools and technical terms of art of
the original operative institution, simply because
of the religious symbolism which these conveyed.
They became the Freemasons of the present day,
and established on an imperishable foundation that
sublime institution which presents all over the hab-

itable earth the most wonderful system of religious and moral symbolism that the world ever saw. The Grand Lodges of York and of London kept up a friendly intercourse and mutual interchange of recognition, until 1725, when dissensions arose from encroachment upon territory, causing opposition to each other, and in 1735 all friendly intercourse ceased. From that time the York Masons considered their interests distinct from the Masons under the Grand Lodge in London. Three years after, in 1738, several brethren, dissatisfied with the conduct of the Grand Lodge of England, seceded from it, and held unauthorized meetings for the purpose of initiation. Taking advantage of the breach between the Grand Lodges of York and London, they assumed the character of the York Masons. On the Grand Lodge's determination to put strictly in execution the laws against such seceders, they still further separated from its jurisdiction and assumed the appellation of "Ancient York Masons." They announced that the ancient landmarks were alone preserved by them; and declaring that the regular Lodges had adopted new plans, and sanctioned innovations, they branded them with the name of "Modern Masons." In 1739 they established a new Grand Lodge in London, under the name of "Grand Lodge of Ancient York Masons," and persevering in the measures they had adopted, held communications and appointed annual feasts. They were soon after recognized by the Masons of Scotland and Ireland, and were encouraged and fostered by many of the nobility. The two Grand Lodges continued to exist, and to act in opposition to each other, extending their schisms into other countries, especially into America, until the year 1813, when, under the Grand Mastership of the Duke of Sussex for the "Moderns" and his brother, the Duke of Kent, for the "Ancients," they were united under the title of the "United Grand Lodge of England." The "Grand Lodge of All England" at York continued to work until 1792, when it finally collapsed.

Such is the history of Freemasonry in England as conceded by all Masons and Masonic writers for the past two centuries. It spread in other countries with more or less activity, for through the instrumentality of the Grand Lodge of England, which became, indeed, the Mother Lodge of the World, Freemasonry was everywhere revived. Lodges on the English model, which afterwards gave rise to the establishment of Grand Lodges in their respective countries, were organized in France in 1727, in Holland in 1731, in Germany in 1733 and in Italy in 1735. Freemasonry was established in America at Boston, Mass., in the year 1733.

Fraternity of Builders or Freemasons of Continental Europe.

GERMANY.

It is universally admitted that in the early ages of Christianity the clergy alone were the patrons of arts and sciences. This was because all learning was then almost exclusively confined to ecclesiastics. Very few of the laity could read or write; even kings affixed the sign of the cross, in place of their signatures, to the charters and other documents which they issued, and from the time of Charlemagne, in the eighth century, to the middle of the twelfth all knowledge and practice of architecture, painting and sculpture were exclusively confined to the monks; and bishops personally superintended the erection of the churches and cathedrals in their dioceses, because not only the principles, but the practice of the art of building, were secrets kept within the walls of cloisters, and were unknown to laymen. Many of the founders of the monastic orders made it a peculiar duty for the monks* to devote themselves to architecture and church building. In the year 716 A. D. the English monk, St. Boniface, went into Germany [1] and organized a special class of monks for the practice of building, under the name of Operarii, or Craftsmen, and Magestri Operum, or Masters of the Works. The labors and duties of these monks were divided and under the same system or organization as the Roman Colleges of Artificers. [2] Some of them designed the plan of the building, others were painters and sculptors, and then there were those who were called cœmentarii, or stonemasons, who performed the practical labors of construction. In large buildings, where many workmen were required, laymen were also employed under the direction of the monks. Among the laymen who were employed in the monasteries as assistants and laborers, many were possessed of superior intelligence. The constant and intimate association of these with the

---

[1] See page 63, first paragraph.

[2] See page 59.

monks in the prosecution of the same design led to
this result: that in the process of time, gradually
and almost unconsciously, the monks imparted to
them the art, secrets and principles of architecture.
Then, by degrees, the knowledge of the arts and
sciences went from these monkish builders out into
the world, and the laymen architects, withdrawing
from the ecclesiastical fraternities, organized
brotherhoods of their own.   These independent
brotherhoods now began to be called upon wherever
an important building was to be erected, and event-
ually they entirely superseded the monkish teachers
in the prosecution of the art of building.   But now
a new classification took place.   The more intelli-
gent of the laymen, who had received these secrets
from the monks, were distinguished as architects
from the ordinary laborers, or common masons.
The latter knew only the use of the trowel and mor-
tar, while the former were occupied in devising
plans for building.   These brotherhoods of high
artists soon won great esteem, and many privileges
and franchises were conceded to them by the munic-
ipal authorities among whom they practiced their
profession.   Their places of assembly were called
Lodges, and the members took the name of *Freemasons.*   Their patron* saint was St. John the Baptist, who was honored by them as the mediator
between the old and the new covenants, and the
first martyr of the Christian religion.   Such was
the beginning of the brotherhoods of Masons in
Germany.

The most important event in the cultivation and
spread of Masonic art on the continent of Europe
was that which occurred at the city of Strasburg in

Germany, when Erwin of Steinbach, the architect of the cathedral, summoned a great number of Master-builders out of Germany, England and Italy, and in the year 1275 established a code of regulations and organized the fraternity of Freemasons after the mode which had been adopted three hundred and fifty years before by the English Masons at the city of York.[1] Three grades of Workmen were recognized—Masters, Fellow Crafts and Apprentices; and words, signs and grips were created as modes of recognition to be used by the members of the fraternity, a part of which was borrowed from the English Masons. Finally, ceremonies of initiation were invented, which were of a symbolic character, and concealed under their symbolism profound doctrines of philosophy, religion and architecture. Lodges were then established in many of the cities of Germany, all of which fraternized with each other. They admitted many eminent persons, and especially ecclesiastics, who were not Operative Masons, but who gave to them their patronage and protection.[2] A Grand Lodge was established at the city of Strasburg, and Erwin of Steinbach was elected their presiding officer, or Grand Master. These fraternities or associations became at once very popular. Many of the potentates of Europe conceded to them considerable powers of jurisdiction, such as would enable them to preserve the most rigid system in matters pertaining to building, and would facilitate them in bringing workmen together at any required point. They

---

[1] See page 64, first paragraph.
[2] Adopted later by the English Fraternities. See page 65.

continued to exist without interruption until 1707, when a decree of the Imperial Diet at Ratisbon dissolved the connection of the Lodges of Germany with the Grand Lodge of Strasburg, because that city had in 1687 passed into the power of the French. The head being now lost, the subordinate bodies began rapidly to decline, and in 1731, by an imperial edict of Charles I., nearly all the Lodges in Germany were dissolved, and lost sight of until the restoration of the Order in the eighteenth century, through the English Fraternity.

FRANCE.

In the beginning of the tenth century a Fraternity of Architects was founded in France, and was similar to that of their German brethren. Originating like them, from the cloisters, and from the employment of laymen by the monkish architects, the connection between the Masons of France and the Roman Colleges of Artificers was more intimate and direct than that of the Germans, because of the early and very general occupation of Gaul by the Roman legions; but the French organizations did not materially differ from the Germans. Protected by popes and princes, the Masons were engaged under ecclesiastical patronage in the construction of religious edifices. The principal seat of the French Fraternity was at Como, a city of Lombardy, from where the Lodges were disseminated over the kingdom, and who passed from country to country and from city to city under the name of "Traveling Freemasons." In the beginning of the sixteenth century the necessity for their employment in further construction of religious edifices having ceased, the fraternity began to decline, and finally in the year 1539 they were dissolved by an edict of Francis I., king of France, and ceased to exist as a recognized system until its revival in the eighteenth century, through the English Fraternity.

ITALY.

In Italy the Association of Architects never entirely ceased to exist, but the greater number of them became connected with the fraternities of France at Como, and were lost sight of.

Conclusion

Freemasonry presents itself under two different aspects: First, as a secret society distinguished by a peculiar ritual; and secondly, as a society having a philosophy on which it is founded, and which it proposes to teach to its disciples. These by way of distinction may be called the ritualistic and philosophical elements of Freemasonry.

The *ritualistic element* of Freemasonry is that which relates to the due performance of the rites and ceremonies of the Order. It belongs entirely to the inner organization of the Institution, or to the manner in which its services shall be conducted, and is interesting or important only to its own members.

The *philosophical element* of Freemasonry is one of much importance. For it, and through it, the Institution is entitled to the respect, and even veneration, of all good men, and is well worth the careful consideration of scholars.

This Society, or Confraternity as it might more appropriately be called, is distinguished from all other associations by the possession of certain symbols, myths, and above all else, a Golden Legend— all of which are directed to the purification of the heart, to the elevation of the mind, to the development of the great doctrine of immortality.

But whence came these symbols, myths and legends? Who invented them? How and why have they been preserved? Looking back into the remotest days of recorded history, we find a priesthood on the banks of the Nile, thousands of years before the light of Christianity dawned upon the world, teaching the existence in a future life by

74

symbols and legends, which convey the lesson in a peculiar mode. And now, after thousands of years have elapsed, we find the same symbolic and legendary method of instruction for the same purpose preserved in the depository of what is comparatively a modern institution. And between these two extremes of the long past and the present now, we find the intervening period occupied by similar associations, succeeding each other from time to time, and spreading over different countries; but all engaged in the same symbolic instruction, with substantially the same symbols and the same mythical history. During this intervening period, we find that the building corporations of the Middle Ages—coming from the Roman Colleges of Architects, as in England,[1] in France,[2] in Italy,[3] and in Germany,[4] from the cloistered brotherhood of monks—devoted themselves principally to the construction of religious edifices. They consisted mainly of architects and skillful operatives, controlled by the highest principles of their art. They were in possession of important professional secrets, were actuated by deep sentiments of religious devotion, and united with themselves in their labors men of learning, wealth and influence.[5] They assumed from the very first the name of Free-Masons.[6] Subsequently, in the beginning of the eighteenth century, they threw off the operative element of their institution, and adopting an entirely speculative character, they became the *Freemasons* of the present day. The best authorities of to-day advance the theory that "Freemasonry is the succes-

---

[1] See page 62.
[2] See page 72.
[3] See page 73.
[4] See page 68.
[5] See pages 65 and 71.
[6] See pages 61 and 70.

sor, with certainty, of the *Building Corporations of the Middle Ages,* and through them, with less certainty, but with great probability, of the *Roman Colleges of Artificers.* Its connection with the *Temple of Solomon as its birthplace* may have been accidental—a mere arbitrary selection by its inventors, and bears, therefore, only an allegorical meaning; or it may be historical." As a brotherhood, composed of Symbolic Masters and Fellows and Apprentices, derived from an association of Operative Masters, Fellows and Apprentices—those building spiritual temples as those built material ones—*its age may not far exceed six hundred[1] years;* but as a secret association, containing within itself the symbolic expression of a religious idea, it connects itself with *all the ancient Mysteries,* which with similar secrecy gave the same symbolic expression to the same religious idea. These Mysteries were not the cradle of Freemasonry; they were only its analogues. In all places where these ancient religious and mystical rites were celebrated, we find the same lesson of eternal life, taught by a legend and inculcated by the representation of an imaginary death and the resurrection of some cherished being, either the object of esteem as a hero, or of devotion as a god. And it is this legend alone, that connects speculative Freemasonry with the ancient Mysteries of Greece, of Syria and of Egypt.

There is no doubt that all Mysteries had one common source; and no doubt Freemasonry has derived its legend, its symbolic mode of instruction, and the lesson for which that instruction was intended, either directly or indirectly, from the same

---

[1] See page 70, last paragraph.

source. And, if we would respect the axioms of historical science, we must say that the *body* came out of the Middle Ages, but that its *spirit* is to be traced to a far remoter period.

The analogy of the legends of the ancient Mysteries and that of the present form of Freemasonry must at once be apparent, and the best historians of the day, even without documentary evidence, view the Temple of Jerusalem and the Masonic Traditions connected with it as a part of the great allegory of Masonry.

The Masonic organization has been moulded into form closely connected with all the events and characteristics of the Solomonic temple, so that now almost all the symbolism of Freemasonry rests upon or is derived from the "House of the Lord" at Jerusalem. So closely are the two connected that to attempt to separate the one from the other would be fatal to the further existence of Freemasonry. Each lodge is and must be a symbol of the Jewish temple, each Master in the chair a representative of the Jewish king, and every Mason a personation of the Jewish workman.

NOTE.—If the reader will review these subjects in the order named and pages given below, he will find that there are sufficient grounds for the above conclusion of the origin, growth and present form of Freemasonry as traced through the Ancient Mysteries, Building of King Solomon's Temple, Roman Colleges of Artificers, Building Corporations of the Middle Ages, and the adoption of Speculative Masonry or present form of Freemasonry.

The commencement of each subject will be designated by a star ☆, ending with ☆☆

Ancient Mysteries, pages 4 and 12.
Building of King Solomon's Temple, pages 41 and 57.
Roman Colleges of Artificers, page 59.
Building Corporations of the Middle Ages, page 62.
Speculative Masonry, page 65.

Revival

The organization of that important body, the Grand Lodge of England, which took place in the city of London in the year 1717, has been always known in Masonic history as the "Revival of Masonry." Anderson, in his first edition of the "Book of Constitutions," containing the History, Ancient Charges and Regulations for the use of Lodges, which was adopted by the Grand Lodge and published in 1723, speaks of the brethren having revived the drooping Lodges of London; but he makes no other reference to the transaction. In his second edition, published in 1738, he is more diffuse, and the account there given is the only authority we possess of the organization made in 1717. Preston and all subsequent writers have of course derived their authority from Anderson.

Degrees

The word *degree,* in its primitive meaning, signifies a *step.* The degrees of Freemasonry are then the steps by which the candidate ascends from a lower to a higher condition of knowledge. It is now the opinion of the best scholars, that the division of the Masonic system into degrees was the work of the revivalists of the beginning of the eighteenth century; that before that period there was but one degree, or rather one common platform of ritualism; and that the division into Masters, Fellows, and Apprentices was simply a division or gradation of ranks, there being but one form of initiation and one catechism for all. The earliest ritual extant, which is contained in the Grand Mystery, published in 1725, makes no reference to any degrees, but gives only what was the common initiation in use about that time. The division of the Masonic system into three degrees, Dr. Mackey says, "must have grown up after the revival in 1717, but in so gradual and imperceptible a manner that it was impossible to fix the precise date of the introduction of each degree. From the old records, it appears to have been about 1721 that the three degrees were introduced, but the second and third were not perfected until 1738. Even as late as 1735 the Entered Apprentice degree contained the most prominent form of initiation, and he who was an apprentice was, for all practical purposes, a Freemason. It was not until repeated improvements, by the adoption of new ceremonies and new regulations, that the degree of Master Mason took the place which it now occupies; having been confined at first to those who had passed the chair." But there is unquestionable evidence that the modes of recognition, the method of government, the legends, and much of the ceremonial of initiation, were in existence among the Operative Masons of the Middle Ages, and were transmitted to the Speculative Masons of the eighteenth century. The work of Anderson, of Desaguliers, and their contemporaries, was to improve and to enlarge, but not to invent. The Masonic system of the present day has been the result of a slow but steady growth, just as the earliest authorized lectures, arranged by Anderson and Desaguliers in 1720, were subsequently modified and enlarged by the successive labors of Clare, of Dunckerley, of Preston and of Hemming. Did Anderson and Desaguliers submit the simple ceremonial which they found at the reorganization of the Grand Lodge in 1717, to a similar modification and enlargement?

Ritual

The mode of opening and closing a Lodge, of conferring the degrees, of installation and other duties, constitutes a system of ceremonies which are called the Ritual. Much of this Ritual is esoteric, and, not being permitted to be committed to writing, is communicated only by oral instruction. In each Masonic jurisdiction it is required by the superintending authority, that the ritual shall be the same; but it differs more or less in the different Rites and jurisdictions. This, however, does not affect the universality of Masonry. The ritual is only the external and extrinsic form. The doctrine of Freemasonry is everywhere the same. But while the ceremonies, or ritual, have varied at different periods, and still vary in different countries, the science and philosophy, the symbolism and the religion of Freemasonry continue, and will continue to be the same wherever true Masonry is practiced.

Rite

The Latin word *ritus,* whence we get the English *rite,* signifies an approved usage or custom, or an external observance. As a Masonic term, it signifies a method of conferring Masonic light by a collection and distribution of degrees. It is, in other words, the method and order observed in the government of a Masonic system.

The original system of Speculative Masonry consisted of the three symbolic degrees. They were at one time the only degrees known to or practiced by the Craft, called therefore, Ancient Craft Masonry. Hence this was the original Rite or approved usage, and so it continued in England until the year 1813, when at the union of the two Grand Lodges the "Holy Royal Arch" (at one time a part of the Master's degree) was declared to be a part of the system; and thus the English, or as it is more commonly called, the York Rite was made legitimately to consist of four degrees. The abstraction of the Royal Arch from the Master's degree and its location as a separate degree, produced that modification of the York Rite which now exists in England, and should properly be called the Modern York Rite, to distinguish it from the Ancient York Rite, which consisted of only three degrees. But in the United States still greater additions have been made to the Rite through the labors of Webb and other lecturers, and the influence insensibly exerted on the Order by the introduction of the Scottish Rite into this country.

On the continent of Europe the organization of new systems began at an early period, and by the invention of what are known as the high degrees, many Rites were established. All of these agreed in one important essential. They were built upon the three symbolic degrees, which, in every instance, constituted the fundamental basis upon which they were erected. They were intended as an expansion and development of the Masonic ideas contained in these degrees. The Apprentice, Fellow Craft, and Master's degrees were the porch through which every initiate was required to pass before he could gain entrance into the inner temple which had been erected by the founders of the rite. They were the text, and the high degrees the commentary. Some of these Rites have lived only with their authors, and died when their parental energy in fostering them ceased to exert itself. The most important of those which have hitherto or still continue to arrest the attention of the Masonic student is the Scottish Rite. This Rite consists of thirty-three degrees, and sprung from the Rite of Perfection, which consisted of twenty-five degrees, the highest of which was "Sublime Prince of the Royal Secret." The Rite of Perfection was created by the "Council of Emperors of the East and West," a body organized at Paris, in 1758. The Scottish Rite, although one of the youngest of the Masonic Rites, is at this day the most popular and the most extensively diffused. Supreme Councils of governing bodies of the Rite are to be found in almost every civilized country of the world, and in many of them it is the only Masonic obedience.[1] It would be impossible to name all the rites of Masonic origin; suffice it to say, that all were founded subsequent to the revival of Masonry in 1717.

[1] Mackey's Encyclopaedia.

The American Modification of the Masonic system or York Rite, which may with propriety be called the American Rite, is divided into three sections, each section being under an appropriate jurisdiction, and are as follows:

I. Symbolic Degrees.—The first three degrees of Freemasonry, namely, those of Entered Apprentice, Fellow Craft, and Master Mason, are known, by way of distinction, as the "symbolic degrees." The term "symbolic" is exclusively confined to the degrees conferred in a Lodge of the three primitive degrees, which Lodge, therefore, whether opened on the first, the second, or the third degree, is always referred to as a "symbolic Lodge." In this country the degrees are conferred under the charter of State Grand Lodges. Symbolism is the prevailing characteristic of these primitive degrees; and it is because all the science and philosophy and religion of Ancient Craft Masonry is thus concealed from the profane but unfolded to the initiates in symbols, that the first three degrees which comprise it are said to be symbolic. Nothing of this kind is to be found in the degrees above and beyond the third, if we except the Royal Arch, which was unnaturally torn from the Master's degree, of which it, as every Masonic student knows, constituted the complement and consummation.

II. Capitular Degrees.—The degrees conferred under the charter of an American Royal Arch Chapter, which are Mark Master, Past Master, Most Excellent Master, and Royal Arch Mason. The capitular degrees are almost altogether founded on and composed of a series of events in Masonic history, and as the information intended to be communicated in these degrees is of an historical character, there can of course be but little room for symbols or for symbolic instruction. These remarks refer exclusively to the Mark and Most Excellent Master's degree, but are not so applicable to the Royal Arch, which is eminently symbolic. The legends of the second Temple, and the lost word, the peculiar legends of that degree, are among the most prominent symbols of the Masonic system.

III. Cryptic Degrees.—The degrees conferred under the charter of an American Council of Royal and Select Masters, which are the Royal Master and Select Master. Some modern ritualists have added to the list the degree of Super-Excellent Master; but this, although often conferred in a Cryptic Council, is not really a Cryptic degree, since its legend has no connection with the Crypt or secret vault.

————————◈————————

Degrees of Freemasonry.

Symbolic Degrees.

ENTERED APPRENTICE.

The first degree of Freemasonry in all the rites is that of Entered Apprentice. Like the lesser mysteries of the ancient initiations, it is a primary degree intended to prepare the candidate for the higher and fuller instructions of the succeeding degrees. It is therefore, although supplying no valuable historical information, replete in its lecture with instructions on the internal structure of the Order, and is typical of youth.

FELLOW CRAFT.

The second degree of Freemasonry in all the rites is that of the Fellow Craft. Like the degree of Apprentice, it is only preparatory to the higher initiation of the Master; and yet it differs essentially from it in its symbolism. For as the first degree was typical of youth, the second is supposed to represent the stage of manhood, and hence the acquisition of science is made its prominent characteristic. While the former is directed in all its symbols and allegorical ceremonies to the purification of the heart, the latter is intended by its lessons to cultivate the reasoning faculties and improve the intellectual powers.

MASTER MASON.

In all the rites of Masonry, no matter how variant may be their organization in the high degrees, the Master Mason constitutes the third degree.

Masonic historians have found much difficulty in settling the question as to the time of the invention and composition of the degree. The theory that at the building of the temple of Jerusalem the Craft were divided into three or even more degrees, being only a symbolic myth, must be discarded in any historical discussion of the subject. The real question at issue is, whether the Master Mason's degree, as a degree, was in existence among the operative Freemasons before the eighteenth century, or whether we owe it to the Revivalists of 1717, and documentary evidence is yet wanting to settle the precise time of its composition, as we now have it. It was originally called the summit of Ancient Craft Masonry. But under the present organization the degree is actually incomplete, because it needs a complement that is only to be supplied in a higher one. Hence its symbolism is necessarily restricted, in its mutilated form, to the first temple and the present life, although it gives assurance of a future one. (See Revival and Degrees, page 78.)

The whole system of Craft Masonry is intended to present the symbolic idea of man passing through the pilgrimage of life. The Entered Apprentice Mason is taught those elementary instructions which are to fit him for further advancement in his profession, just as the youth is supplied with that rudimentary education which is to prepare him for the active duties of life; as a Fellow Craft he is directed to continue his investigations in the science of the institution and to labor diligently in the tasks it prescribes, just as the man is required to enlarge his mind by the acquisition of new ideas, and to extend his usefulness to his fellow-creatures;

but as a Master Mason he is taught the last, the most important, and the most necessary of truths, that having been faithful to all his trusts, he is at last to die, and to receive the reward of his fidelity. It was the single object of all the ancient rites and mysteries, practiced in the very bosom of pagan darkness, shining as a solitary beacon to all that surrounding gloom, and cheering the philosopher in his weary pilgrimage of life, to teach the immortality of the soul. *This* is still the **great design** of the Third Degree of Masonry.

Capitular Degrees.

MARK MASTER.

Mark Master is the fourth degree of the American rite. The traditions of the degree make it of great historical importance, as we are informed that at the building of the temple each Operative Mason was distinguished by his *mark,* and the disorder and confusion that might otherwise have attended so immense an undertaking was completely prevented. Not less useful is it in its symbolical signification. It teaches us that we should discharge all the duties of our several stations with precision and punctuality; that the work of our hands and the thoughts of our hearts should be good and true, not sinful and defective, not unfinished and imperfect, but such as the Great Overseer and Judge of heaven and earth will see fit to approve as a worthy oblation from his creatures. It holds forth to the desponding the encouraging thought that although our motives may sometimes be misinterpreted by our erring fellow-mortals, our attainments be underrated and our reputations be traduced by the envious and the malicious, there is One, at least, who sees not with the eyes of men, but may yet make the stone which the builders rejected the head of the corner.

PAST MASTER.

The conferring of this degree, which has no historical connection with the rest of the degrees in a chapter, arises from the following circumstances. Originally, when Chapters of Royal Arch Masonry were under the government of Lodges, in which the degree was there always conferred, it was part of the Regulations that no one could receive the Royal Arch degree unless he had previously presided in the Lodge as Master. When the Chapters became independent the regulation could not be abolished, for that would have been an innovation. The difficulty has therefore been obviated by making every candidate for the degree of Royal Arch a Past Master before his exaltation.

MOST EXCELLENT MASTER.

Most Excellent Master, the sixth degree in the American rite. Its history refers to the dedication of the temple of King Solomon, who is represented by its presiding officer under the title of Most Excellent. It is peculiarly American, being practiced in no other country. It was the invention of Webb, who organized the Capitular system of Masonry as it exists in this country, and established the system of lectures which is the foundation of all subsequent systems taught in America.

ROYAL ARCH.

If we except the Master's, there is no other degree in Masonry that has been so extensively diffused, or is as important in its historical and symbolical import, as the Royal Arch, or, as it has been called on account of its sublime significance, the "Holy Royal Arch," the root, the heart and marrow of Masonry. The Master's degree in its symbolic signification is imperfect and unfinished in its history, and, terminating abruptly in its symbolism, it leaves the mind still waiting for something that is necessary to its completeness. This deficiency is supplied by the Royal Arch degree.

The Royal Arch did not exist as an independent and distinctive degree until about the year 1740, when the body which called itself the "Grand Lodge of Ancient York Masons," [1] dissevered the essential element of the Royal Arch from the Master's degree, and invested it with the form of a distinct degree. Previous to this, it was but a complementary part of the Master's degree, to which it gave a necessary completion. In 1776, a similar degree, established by Thos. Dunckerly, was adopted by the Constitutional Grand Lodge, or the "Moderns," and at the union of the two Grand Lodges in 1813, the Royal Arch was formally and officially recognized as a part of the York Rite or Ancient Craft Masonry. In America, as most of the Lodges derived their warrants from the so-called "Grand Lodge of Ancient York Ma-

[1] See page 67.

sons," the Royal Arch must have been introduced at the time of their constitution. The government of the degree was for a long time under the Master's Lodges, and many years elapsed before it was placed under the control of distinct bodies called Grand Chapters. In America the first Grand Chapter was formed in the year 1798. The true symbolism of the Royal Arch system is founded on the discovery of the "Lost Word." That word is, in Masonry, the symbol of TRUTH. This truth, which Masonry makes the great object of its investigations, is not the mere truth of science or the truth of history, but it is the more important truth which is synonymous with the knowledge of the nature of God, that truth which is embraced in the sacred omnific name, including in its signification His eternal present, past and future existence, and to which He himself alluded when He declared to Moses, "I appeared unto Abraham, unto Isaac, and unto Jacob by the name of God Almighty; but by my name Jehovah was I not known unto them." The discovery of the truth is, then, the essential symbolism of the Royal Arch degree.

Captivity.

The historical connection between the building and dedication of the first temple, as found in the Master's and Most Excellent degrees, its destruction, and that subsequent part which smybolizes the building of the second, there is an interval in the ceremonials of the Royal Arch degree. This interval represents the time passed in the captivity of the Jews at Babylon. In 626 B. C. the empire and city of Babylon was conquered by Nabopolassar, a trusted Assyrian general of King Sarsacus of Assyria. He was born of a nomadic race and his home was in the Caucasian mountains. He turned traitor after becoming viceroy of Babylon, and joined forces with Cyaxares, king of Media, and overthrew the Assyrians. The empire was broken up and each of the confederates took his allotted portion. Assyria proper fell to the Medes, and Nabopolassar received the kingdom of Babylon, to which were annexed Susiana on the east, and the valley of the Euphrates and the whole of Syria on the west.

In the year 610 B. C. Pharaoh Necho of Egypt invades Syria and captures Jerusalem, and makes Jehoiakim king of Judah. Nabopolassar, alarmed by the loss of Syria, determines to recover what Necho has taken from him. After the army was raised and equipped, however, the aged king found himself unable to conduct the expedition, and so the command was given to his son Nebuchadnezzar. The prince pushed boldly into upper Syria, where the Egyptians had established themselves in full force to hold the country, and completely routed them. Every vestige of Egyptian resistance melted away. Proceeding towards the west, he paused for a short time in Palestine, where he received the submission of Jehoiakim, whom Pharaoh Necho had set up, and then continued his triumphant course to the gateway of Egypt. It was during this expedition, in the year 606 B. C., that Daniel and his friends were made captives at Jerusalem and taken to Babylon, with many of the sacred vessels. And from this date the principal computation of the seventy years of captivity begins.

Nebuchadnezzar while at the gateway of Egypt receives news of his father's death, and, without delay, he, fearing that some rival might usurp the throne of Babylon, gave orders for his army to retrace its course into upper Syria, and himself, with a detachment, made all speed by the nearest route across the desert to the capital. Upon his arrival he was given a triumphant reception, and was peacefully established on the throne of the empire. His accession, in 604 B. C., marks the era of Babylonian greatness, before whose victorious armies many nations fell. At times insurrections would break forth. Among the first and most important was the revolt of Tyre, the chief city of the Phœnicians. About the same time Jehoiakim, king of Judah—doubtless calling to mind that he owed his own sovereignty to Pharaoh Necho, the rival king of Babylon, and believing that the Egyptians would come to his aid—revolted and took up arms. It was to punish these Phœnicians and Jewish rebels that Nebuchadnezzar undertook the first great campaign after his accession. He invested Tyre, but that strong city proved for a long time impregnable. So the king, without desisting from the siege, divided his forces and with one division proceeded against Jerusalem. To the last moment Jehoiakim relied upon the Egyptians to come to his aid, but the Pharaoh held aloof, and Jehoiakim was left to his fate. He made his submission to Nebuchadnezzar, who deliberately put him to death, and he was "buried with the burial of an ass, drawn and cast forth beyond the gates of Jerusalem." For the time being, the Babylonian king conferred the crown of Judah upon Jehoiachin, son of the recent ruler; but he soon fell under the suspicion of treachery, was deposed and taken captive to Babylon, thus making way for Zedekiah, who was put upon the Jewish throne. For some reason the Jewish people had come to prefer the Egyptian to Babylonian masters. Perhaps they hoped ultimately to throw off all mastery and become independent, as in the days of David. At any rate, Zedekiah, after having kept his faith with Nebuchadnezzar for eight years, became at heart disloyal, and in 588 B. C. entered into an intrigue with Egypt against the Babylonians. When Nebuchadnezzar heard of the revolt, he marched with his host against the city of the Jews, and Jerusalem fell. The city was leveled with the ground, the temple pillaged and burned, and the inhabitants carried captive to Babylon. The state of Judah was extinguished. Gedaliah* was appointed by Nebuchadnezzar to rule over the ruins of Palestine, among which Jeremiah sat weeping. That captivity lasted for fifty-two years, and is commemorated in the Royal Arch degree. It was a part of the "seventy years' captivity" of the Jews, which was foretold by the prophet Jeremiah, the beginning of which, however, as has been mentioned, commenced eighteen years before.

Among the prisoners of distinction was the high priest and the priest that was next to him, with the three rulers that guarded the temple, the eunuch who was over the armed men, seven friends of Zedekiah, his scribe and two other rulers. Zedekiah the king attempted to escape previous to the termination of the siege, but was pursued, captured, and carried to the headquarters of Nebuchadnezzar, who was then at Riblah,* where, having first been compelled to behold the slaughter of his children, his eyes were put out, and he was conducted in chains to Babylon. On the arrival of the captives

CAPTIVE JEWS LED INTO BABYLONIA.

at Babylon they do not appear to have been subjected to the extreme rigors of slavery. They were distributed into the various part of the empire, some remaining in the city, while others were sent into the provinces. They were permitted to retain their personal property and even to purchase lands and erect houses. Their civil and religious government was not utterly destroyed, for they kept up a regular succession of kings and high priests. Some of the principal captives were advanced to offices of dignity and power in the royal palace, and were permitted to share in the councils of state.

Jehoiachin, who was the first king of Judea carried captive to Babylon, was succeeded by his son Shealtiel, and he by his son Zerubbabel, who was the head of the captivity or nominal prince of Judea at the close of the captivity. Jehosadek was the high priest carried by Nebuchadnezzar to Babylon, where he died during the captivity and was succeeded by his eldest son, Joshua.

Babylon the Great, as the prophet Daniel calls it, was situated 475 miles in a nearly easterly direction from Jerusalem. It stood in the midst of a large and fertile plain on each side of the river Euphrates, which ran through it from north to south, the original foundation of which was Babel. Babel was also the name of a lofty tower, which the descendants of Noah began to build, among whom Nimrod was a leader, about one hundred and twenty years after the flood, so called because God there confounded the language of those who were employed in the undertaking (Gen. x. 10; xi. 9). Their object in building the city and tower was to concentrate the population and the dominion at that spot; and as this was contrary to the divine purpose of replenishing the earth with inhabitants, and betrayed an ungodly and perhaps idolatrous disposition, God frustrated their designs by miraculously giving to different portions of the people different languages or different modes of pronunciation and divergent dialects of the original language of man,

thus causing them to disperse over the globe
(Acts ii. 1-11). The tower was apparently left
incomplete, but the foundation of the city was
probably laid, and a portion no doubt of the
builders continued to dwell there. The, place
became afterwards the celebrated city of Bay-
ylon. It has been supposed that the Tower of

BABYLON.

Babel was afterwards finished and called the Tower
of Belus within the city of Babylon. Herodotus
visited this tower, and describes it as a square pyramid, measuring half a mile in circumference at
the base; from this rose eight towers, one above
another, gradually decreasing to the summit, which
was reached by a broad road winding up around
the outside. This tower was used for astronomical
purposes, but was chiefly devoted to the worship
of Bel, whose temple contained immense treasures,

including several statues of massive gold, one of which was forty feet in height. Here were deposited the sacred golden vessels brought from Jerusalem. Babylon reached the summit of her greatness and splendor under Nebuchadnezzar, the son and sucessor of Nabopolassar. The city was surrounded with walls which were eighty-seven feet thick, three hundred and fifty feet in height and sixty miles in compass. These were all built of large bricks cemented together with bitumen. Exterior to the walls was a wide and deep trench lined with the same material. Twenty-five gates on each side made of solid brass gave admission to the city. From each of these gates proceeded a wide street fifteen miles in length, and the whole was separated by means of smaller divisions, and contained 676 squares, each of which was two miles and a quarter in circumference. Two hundred and fifty towers placed upon the walls afforded the means of additional strength and protection. Within this immense circuit were to be found palaces and temples and other edifices of the utmost magnificence, which have caused the wealth, the luxury and the splendor of Babylon to become a favorite theme of the historians of antiquity. It is scarcely too much to say that but for Nebuchadnezzar the Babylonians would have had no place in history. At any rate, their actual place is owing almost entirely to this prince, who to the military talents of an able general added a grandeur of artistic conception and a skill in construction which place him on a par with the greatest builders of antiquity. After he captured Jerusalem and burned the great Temple of Solomon and carried away the Jews as captives to Babylon, he also took Tyre and conquered Egypt, and became without doubt the most powerful monarch of his time. He promoted the Hebrew prophet Daniel to the second place in the kingdom. He died in 562 B. C., and was succeeded by his son, Evil-Merodach, who reigned only two years. (For an account of Nebuchadnezzar's character, his marvelous experience, his loss of reason, and his restoration, the reader is referred to the Book of Daniel.) Nabonadius ascended the throne in 555 B. C., as the sixth king in the line of Nabopolassar, and appears to have shared the royal power with his son Belshazzar,* whose mother was the daughter of Nebuchadnezzar.

The location of Babylon gave her to a great extent the control of the traffic, by the Euphrates and by caravans, between central Asia and Arabia and Egypt; and into her lap flowed, either through conquest or commerce, the wealth of almost all known lands. In consequence of the opulence and luxury of the inhabitants, corruptness and licentiousness of manners and morals were carried to a frightful extreme.

Termination of the Captivity.

In the year 538 B. C., Cyrus, king of Persia, a great conqueror, who had reduced nearly all Asia, crossed the Euphrates and laid siege to Babylon, which he took after two years by diverting the course of the river Euphrates from its channel by digging a canal, which ran west of the city, and carried off the superfluous water of the Euphrates into Lake Nitocris, which by this means was rendered so shallow that his soldiers were able to penetrate along its bed into the city. He made his successful assault on a night when the whole city, relying on the strength of the walls, had given themselves up

CYRUS THE GREAT.

to the riot and debauchery of a grand festival and the king and his nobles were reveling at a splendid entertainment. Prince Belshazzar and his nobles were slain at their banquet, and the dawn found the victorious Persians in complete possession of the city. Nabonadius, the Babylonian king, was at Bor-

sippa with part of his army, where he surrendered
to Cyrus under honorable terms, Cyrus bestowing
on the dethroned king the governorship of the
province of Carmania. Cyrus constitutes his uncle
"Darius the Median"* king of Babylon, who
reigned two years till the time of his death. During

CAPTURE OF BABYLON.

his reign Daniel was cast into the lions' den (Dan.
vi.). In 536 B. C., Cyrus succeeded to the whole
empire, and in the first year of his reign the Jewish
captivity terminated. Cyrus, from his conversa-
tions with Daniel and other Jewish captives of
learning and piety, as well as from the perusal of
their sacred books, more especially the prophecies
of Isaiah, had become imbued with a knowledge of

true religion, and made a public announcement to his subjects of his belief in the God "which the nations of the Israelites worshiped." He was consequently impressed with an earnest desire to fulfill the prophetic declarations of which he was the subject and to rebuild the Temple of Jerusalem. Cyrus, therefore, issued a decree by which the Jews were permitted to return to Jerusalem. Zerubbabel, the prince of Judah, was the grandson of that king (Jehoiachin) who had been deposed by Nebuchadnezzar and carried captive to Babylon. In him, therefore, was vested the regal authority, and on him, as such, the command of the returning captives was bestowed by Cyrus, who on that occasion, according to Masonic tradition, presented to him the sword which Nebuchadnezzar had received from his grandfather. He also restored to him the greater part of the sacred vessels of the temple which had been carried away by Nebuchadnezzar, the remainder being brought back many years after by Ezra.

Only 42,360 Israelites, exclusive of servants and slaves, accompanied Zerubbabel, out of whom he selected 7,000 of the most valiant, whom he placed as an advance guard at the head of the people. Their progress homeward was not altogether unattended with danger; for tradition informs us that at the river Euphrates they were opposed by the Assyrians, who, incited by the temptation of the vast amount of golden vessels which they were carrying, drew up in hostile array, and, notwithstanding the remonstrances of the Jews and the edict of Cyrus, disputed their passage. Zerubbabel, however, repulsed the enemy with such ardor as to ensure a signal victory, most of the Assyrians having been slain in the battle or drowned in their attempt to cross the river in their retreat. The remainder of the journey was uninterrupted, and after a march of four months, which took them through the ruins of Rabbah* and old Tadmor,* or Palmyra of the desert, and the ruins of Damascus,* Zerubbabel arrived at Jerusalem with his followers in the month of June, 535 B. C.

During their captivity the Jews continued to practice the rites of Masonry, and established, at various places, regular Lodges in Chaldea.* According to the Rabbinical traditions, they instituted their mystic fraternity at Naharda on the Euphrates, and Zerubbabel carried with him to Jerusalem all the secret knowledge which was the property of that institution, and established a similar fraternity in Judea. This coincides with and gives additional strength to the traditions of the Royal Arch degree. As soon as the pious pilgrims had arrived at Jerusalem and taken a needful rest of seven days, a tabernacle for the temporary purposes of divine worship was erected near the ruins of the ancient temple, and a council was called, in which Zerubbabel presided as king, Jeshua as high priest, and Haggai as scribe, or principal officer of state. It was there determined to commence the building of the second temple upon the same holy spot which had been occupied by the first, and the people contributed nearly a quarter of a million of dollars toward paying the expenses.

Scarcely had the workmen well commenced their labors when they were interrupted by the Samaritans, who made application to be permitted to unite with them in the construction of the temple. But the Jews, who looked upon them as idolaters, refused to accept their services. The Samaritans in consequence became bitter enemies and so prevailed, by misrepresentations, with the ministers of

REBUILDING JERUSALEM.

Cyrus, as to cause them to put such obstructions in the way of construction of the edifice as to seriously impede its progress for several years. (See Cyrus, in Supplement.)

In the seventh year after the restoration of the Jews, Cyrus, their friend and benefactor, died (530 B. C.), and was succeeded by his son Cambyses (Ahasuerus), who, after a reign of eight years, died in Syria. Smerdis, called in Scripture Artaxerxes, then usurped the throne of Persia, and forbade the Jews to proceed with the work, and the temple re-

mained in an unfinished state until his death, and
the succession of Darius to the throne (521 B. C.).
As in early life there had been a great intimacy between this sovereign and Zerubbabel, the latter proceeded to Babylon and obtained permission from the
monarch to resume the labor. Zerubbabel returned
to Jerusalem, and notwithstanding some further delays consequent upon the enmity of the neighboring
nations, the second temple, or, as it may be called
by way of distinction from the first, the Temple
of Zerubbabel, was completed in the sixth year of
the reign of Darius, 515 B. C., just twenty years
after its commencement. It was then dedicated
with all the solemnities that accompanied the dedication of the first. (See Darius, king of Persia,
in Supplement.)

Zerubbabel was of the royal race of David, and
called "Sheshbazzar the prince of Judah." He was
born in Babylon, as his name imports, but nothing
further than what has been said is known of his
history except that from him both Joseph and Mary
descended.

The general plan of this second temple was similar to that of the first, but it exceeded it in almost
every dimension by one-third. The decorations of
gold and other ornaments in the first temple must
have far surpassed those bestowed upon the second,
for we are told by Josephus (Antiq. xi. 4) that "the
priests and Levites and elders of families were dis-
consolate at seeing how much more sumptuous the
old temple was than the one which, on account of
their poverty, they had just been able to erect." (See
Jerusalem, in Supplement.)

Cryptic Degrees.

Council of Royal and Select Masters.

The proper jurisdiction under which these degrees should be placed, whether under Chapters and to be conferred preparatory to the Royal Arch degree, or under Councils and to be conferred after it, has excited discussion. The former usage prevails in Maryland and Virginia, but the latter in all the other States. There is no doubt that these degrees belonged originally to the Ancient and Accepted Scottish Rite, and were conferred as honorary degrees by the Inspectors of that Rite. Repeated attempts have been made to take the degrees out of the hands of the Councils and to place them in Chapters, there to be conferred as preparatory to the Royal Arch.

The General Grand Chapter, in the triennial session of 1847, adopted a resolution granting this permission to all Chapters in States where no Grand Councils exist. But, seeing the manifest injustice and inexpediency of such a measure, in 1853 it disclaimed all control over them, and forbade the Chapters under its jurisdiction to confer them. As far as regards the interference of the Ancient and Accepted Scottish Rite, that question was set at rest in 1870 by the Mother Council, which, at its session at Baltimore, formally relinquished all further control over them.

ROYAL MASTER.

The eighth degree of the American Rite, and the first of the degrees conferred in a Council of Royal and Select Masters. The place of meeting is called the "Council Chamber," and represents the private apartment of King Solomon, in which he is said to have met for consultation with his two colleagues during the construction of the Temple. Candidates who receive this degree are said to be "honored with the degree of Royal Master."

From the legendary history and the symbolism of the degree, we find that, brief and simple as are the ceremonies, they present the great Masonic idea of the laborer seeking for his reward. Throughout all the symbolism of Masonry, from the first to the last degree, the search for the WORD has been considered but as a symbolic expression for the search after TRUTH. The attainment of this truth has always been acknowledged to be the great object and design of all Masonic labor. Divine truth—the knowledge of God—concealed in the old Kabalistic doctrine, under the symbol of His ineffable name, and typified in the Masonic system under the mystical expression of the True Word, is the reward proposed to every Mason who has faithfully wrought his task. It is, in short, the "Master's wages."

SELECT MASTER.

The ninth degree in the American Rite, and the second of the degrees conferred in a Council of Royal and Select Masters. A Council is supposed to consist of neither more nor less than twenty-seven; but a smaller number, if not less than nine, is competent to proceed to work or business. The candidate, when initiated, is said to be "chosen as a Select Master." The historical object of the degree is to commemorate the deposit of an important secret or treasure which, after the preliminary preparation, is said to have been made by Hiram Abif. The place of meeting represents a secret vault beneath the Temple.

SUPER EXCELLENT MASTER

A degree which was originally an honorary or side degree conferred by the Inspectors-General of the Ancient and Accepted Scottish Rite at Charleston. It has since been introduced into some of the Royal and Select Councils of the United States, and there conferred as an additional degree. The degree is simply an enlargement of that part of the ceremonies of the Royal Arch which refer to the Temple destruction. It has nothing to do with the ideas inculcated in Cryptic Masonry. Whence the degree originally sprang, it is impossible to tell. As to the symbolic design of the degree, it is very evident that its legend and ceremonies are intended to inculcate that important Masonic virtue—fidelity to vows.

BOOK OF THE LAW

By an ancient usage of the Craft, the Holy Bible, or Book of the Law, is always spread open in the Lodge. There is in this, as in everything else that is Masonic, an appropriate symbolism. The Book of the Law is the Great Light of Masonry. To close it would be to intercept the rays of divine light which emanate from it; and hence it is spread open, to indicate that the Lodge is not in darkness, but under the influence of its illuminating power. Masons in this respect obey the suggestion of the Divine Founder of the Christian religion, "Neither do men light a candle and put it under a bushel, but on a candlestick; and it giveth light unto all that are in the house."

Masonically, the Book of the Law is that sacred

book which is believed by the Mason of any par
ticular religion to contain the revealed will of God.
And therefore, whatever to any people expresses
that will may be used as a substitute for the Bible
in a Masonic Lodge. Thus, to the Christian Mason
the Book of the Law is the Old and New Testaments; to the Jew, the Old Testament; to the Mus-
sulman, the Koran; to the Brahman, the Vedas;
and to the Parsee, the Zendavesta. They all convey the same idea—that of the symbolism of the
Divine will revealed to man.

Freemasonry alone has no secret doctrine. Its
philosophy is open to the world. Its modes of recognition by which it secures identification, and its
rites and ceremonies, which are its method of instruction, alone are secret. All men may know the
tenets of the Masonic creed. This creed consists
of two articles: First, a belief in God, the Creator
of all things, who is therefore recognized as the
Grand Architect of the Universe; and secondly,
a belief in the eternal life, to which this present life
is but a preparatory and probationary state.

At the revival of Masonry in 1717, the Grand
Lodge of England set forth the Law, as to the religious creed to be required of a Mason in the following words, to be found in the charges approved
by that body: "In ancient times, Masons were
charged in every country to be of the religion of
that country or nation, whatever it was; yet it is
now thought more expedient only to oblige them
to that religion in which all men agree, leaving their
particular opinions to themselves."

This is now considered universally as the recognized law on the subject.

Design of Freemasonry.

The "Design of Freemasonry" is neither charity nor almsgiving, nor the cultivation of social sentiments; for both of these are merely incidental to its organization. But it is the search after *truth*, and that *truth* is the *unity of God and the immortality of the soul*. The various degrees or grades of initiation represent the various stages through which the human mind passes, and the many difficulties which men, individually and collectively, must encounter in their progress from ignorance to the acquisition of *truth*. That truth lies concealed in its symbols, and these, constituting, as they do, a picture language, or art speech, are made to carry a complete philosophy of the existence and relations of Deity, nature and man.

Freemasonry is not only a universal science, but a world-wide religion,[1] and owes allegiance to no one creed, and can adopt no sectarian dogma, as such, without ceasing thereby to be Masonic. Drawn from the Kabbalah,[2] and taking the Jewish or Christian verbiage or symbols, it but discerns in them universal truths, which it recognizes in all other religions. Freemasonry is not Christianity, nor a substitute for it. It is not intended to supersede it nor any other form of worship or system of faith. Its religion is that general one of nature and primitive revelations, handed down to us from some ancient and patriarchal priesthood, in which all men may agree and in which no men

---

[1] See Religion of Masonry, in Supplement.
[2] See Kabbalah, in Supplement.

can differ. It inculcates the practice of virtue,
but it supplies no scheme of redemption for sin.
It points its disciples to the path of righteousness,
but it does not claim to be "the way, the truth,
and the life." Neither persecution nor misrepre-
sentation can ever destroy it. It may find no place
in a generation of bigots; it may retire for a century; but again comes a Master Builder with the
key to the "shut palace of the King," throws open
the blinds, lets in the light, kindles anew the fire
on the sacred altar, clears away the rubbish, when
behold! the tesselated pavement is as bright as
when it first came from the quarries of truth, the
jewels are of pure gold and brightens at the touch,
and the great lights are undimmed and undecayed.
"When the candidate is ready, the Master appears."
And yet men are so foolish as to imagine that
they can destroy this heirloom of the ages; this
heritage from the Immortals! No age is so dark
as to quench entirely the light of the Lodge; no
persecution so bloody as to blot out its votaries;
no edict so lasting as to count one second on its
Dial of Time! These, one and all, serve only to
keep the people in darkness, and retard the reign
of universal brotherhood.

Commandery.
Knights Templar.

In the United States an assembly of Knights Templar is called a Commandery, and must consist of at least nine members. The government of Masonic Knights Templar in this country is vested, first, in Commanderies, which confer the degrees of Knight of the Red Cross, Knights Templar, and Knight of Malta.

Commanderies are under the control of Grand Commanderies in States in which those bodies exist. Where they do not, the warrants are derived directly from the Grand Encampment. The supreme authority of the Order is exercised by the Grand Encampment of the United States, which meets triennially. The presiding officer is a Grand Master.

The Ancient Order of Knights Templar was divided into Provinces, each of which was governed by a Grand Preceptor or Grand Prior. These Provinces were fifteen in number and extended from Jerusalem to England. There was no part of Europe, except the impoverished Kingdoms of Denmark, Sweden and Norway, where the Templars had not extended their possessions and their influence.

In all the Provinces there were numerous temple-houses called Preceptories, presided over by a Preceptor. Some of the houses were also called Commanderies. The latter name has been adopted by the Masonic Templars of this country.

Knight of the Red Cross.

This degree, whose legend dates it far anterior to the Christian era and in the reign of Darius, has no analogy with the chivalric orders of knighthood. It is purely Masonic and intimately connected with the Royal Arch degree. In this country it is always conferred in a Commandery of Knights Templar and is given as a preliminary reception in that degree. The legend is as follows: "After the death of Cyrus, the Jews, who had been released by him from their captivity and permitted to return to Jerusalem for the purpose of rebuilding the temple, found themselves obstructed in the undertaking by the neighboring nations and especially by the Samaritans. Hereupon they sent an embassy, at the head of which was their prince, Zerubbabel, to Darius, the successor of Cyrus, to crave his interposition and protection. Zerubbabel, awaiting a favorable opportunity, succeeded not only in obtaining his request, but also in renewing the friendship which had formerly existed between the king and himself.[1] In commemoration of these

---

[1] See page 104.

events, Darius is said to have instituted a new Order and called it the Knights of the East. They afterwards assumed their present name from the red cross borne in their banners."

Knights Templar.

In the early centuries of our era the Semitic race sent forth to the nations two great streams of religion; and out of this contribution sprang the rival systems of Christianity and Mohammedanism. Each would be all or nothing. Each entered into combination with the political structure of states, and sought by means of the temporal power, or open proclamation of its own right, to control the institutions and sway the destinies of the world. In the struggle which ensued, the powers of primitive civilization were arrayed against each other under the Cross and the Crescent. In the issue Europe fell to Christ; Asia and Africa, to Mohammed.

The Cross.

Christianity Was Conceived in Abraham and Given Birth through Jesus Christ.

Abraham,* originally Abram, was the founder of the Jewish nation, and was born at Ur, in Mesopotamia, in 1996 B. C. He marries Sarah, and in 1922 B. C. removes to Haran in Mesopotamia. A few years later they go to the land of Canaan, and there, in 1896 B. C., in their extreme old age,[1] Isaac is born. At the age of forty Isaac marries Rebekah, and in 1836 B. C. twin sons were born whom they called Jacob and Esau.

Jacob, in 1753 B. C., marries Leah and Rachel and has six sons and one daughter by Leah: Reuben, Simeon, Levi, Judah, Issachar, Zebulun, and Dinah; two sons by Rachel's handmaid, Bilhah: Dan and Naphtali; two by Zilpah, Leah's handmaid: Gad and Asher; two by Rachel: Joseph and Benjamin. The twelve sons of Jacob became the immediate ancestors of the twelve tribes of Israel.

In 1571 B. C. there came into the world that great lawgiver, Moses, the first prophet of Israel. He was the son of Amram and Jochebed, of the tribe of Levi, and the youngest brother of Miriam and Aaron. The name of Moses is one of the greatest in history. He organized the Hebrew people; he formed the Hebrew character; and the influence which the Hebrew nation has exercised on the civilization of mankind, by being through many centuries the bearer of the monotheistic idea, can hardly be overestimated. For many generations the Jews had lived in the most abject thralldom;

---

[1] See page 20, first paragraph.

they had lost all feeling of independence and self-confidence, and the peculiarities of their race were contaminated and perverted, instead of having been developed into a national character; they were utterly unfit for the conquest of a country, for the organization of a state, and for the part they were destined to play in history.

According to the Biblical narrative (Acts vii.), Moses was forty years old when he fled from Egypt into Arabia, eighty when he returned and led the march across the Red Sea to Sinai, and 120 when he died on Mount Nebo. Under his leadership the Hebrew people, during their forty years of penal wandering in the desert, took on the religious and moral character which enabled them to begin their career in Palestine.

Judah, one of the twelve patriarchs, and the progenitor of the tribe of the same name, became so predominant in Palestine as to give its name to the kingdom of Judea and ultimately to the whole race of the descendants of Abraham (Jews). Judah appears to have exercised a kind of leadership among his brothers; it was he who persuaded them not to kill Joseph, but to sell him to the Midianites, and on the journey to Egypt to buy corn it was Judah who acted as spokesman for the whole company. As such he offered himself to Joseph as a slave to ransom his half-brother Benjamin. He married a Canaanite woman, by whom he had three sons: Er, Onan and Shelah. Er and Onan died in the land of Canaan without issue. Tamar, his daughter-in-law, through deceit, bore him twin sons, Pharez and Zarah (Gen. xxxviii.), from the first of whom David, and ultimately Christ, were descended. Of the life of Judah in Egypt nothing is known except that he was still living at the time of his father's death, and received that splendid blessing which foretold the glory of his lineage (Gen. xlix. 8-12).

Judaism, the religious system and polity of the

JESUS.

Jews, as enjoined in the laws of Moses, became the basis of a spiritual or universal religion.

"And she [Mary] shall bring forth a son, and thou shalt call his name JESUS: for he shall save his people from their sins" (Matt. i. 21; Luke i. 31-33).

Jesus the Christ was born in Bethlehem, a small Judean town, already famous as the birthplace of

King David, and about six miles south of Jerusalem. The home of his mother, Mary, was Nazareth in Galilee, but she had come to Bethlehem with her husband, Joseph, a descendant of David, in obedience to a decree of enrollment and taxation which seems to have required Joseph's presence at the original home of his family. Mary is thought to have been, like Joseph, descended from the royal house of Judah. Jesus is supposed to have been born on the 25th of December, four years before the year 1 A. D. On the eighth day after his birth he was circumcised, and on the fortieth day he was taken to the temple, when the customary offerings of purification were made by his mother. The visit of certain "wise men," or magians, who came probably from Persia, to the infant at Bethlehem, with gifts proper for a king, and the inquiries made by them previously at Jerusalem for a newly born king of the Jews, excited the jealousy of Herod the Great, then ruling over Judea and the neighboring territories under the protection of the Romans, and he issued orders for a massacre of young children at Bethlehem. Joseph, being warned, took the young child and his mother by night and fled into Egypt in time to escape the destruction, where they remained until again warned of Herod's death a short time after. Joseph seems to have intended to rear the child at Bethlehem (the city of David), but another warning caused him to return to Nazareth. Twelve years later Joseph and Mary took Jesus with them to Jerusalem to keep the Passover, and he then showed that he was already conscious of a divine mission. He lived at Nazareth, however, for eighteen years longer, and probably assisted Joseph at his trade, that of carpenter. Joseph is not mentioned again in the Gospels, and is supposed to have died before Christ entered on his public labors.

When Jesus was about thirty years old, his kinsman, John, the son of Zacharias, began to announce the near approach of the kingdom of God and to call his countrymen to prepare for it by a moral reformation, and by accepting baptism at his hands as a sign of the remission of sin. Jesus appeared among the throngs which gathered about John the Baptist at the Jordan, and insisted on being baptized by him. After John had reluctantly administered the rite to one whom he felt by a kind of prophetic instinct, as it would seem, to be holier than himself, he was shown that Jesus was the Messiah, the Son of God, and he announced him as such to those about him. After his baptism a few of John's disciples attached themselves to Jesus, and accompanied him to Galilee. He then went to Jerusalem and began his public ministry and announced himself to the heads of the nation there as a messenger of Heaven, by expelling from the temple court those who had been allowed to carry on traffic in it for the convenience of worshipers. One member of the Sanhedrim,* Nicodemus,* became at this time a secret adherent of the new prophet. For a few months Jesus carried on a work in Judea similar to that in which John the Baptist was engaged, and seemed to be co-operating with the latter in the effort to bring about a national repentance. But as attempts were being made to create dissension between his followers and those of John, he retired to Galilee.

After John the Baptist was put to death by Herod Antipas, Governor of Galilee, Jesus began his second and final attempt to gain a hearing from the representatives of the nation at Jerusalem. He appeared somewhat suddenly at the feast of tabernacles,* and by miracles and discourses, as well as by the angry opposition which he excited, he at least succeeded in awakening new interest in his movements, and fixing the attention of the nation upon himself during the rest of his career. For several years after this he carried on his teachings throughout Palestine, meeting with much opposition and many trials and tribulations. The rulers began to fear his growing popularity and about the year 29, when he was returning to Bethany * from Jerusalem, he was betrayed by Judas, arrested and led back to the city for trial before the Sanhedrim. The charge was blasphemy, but in the absence of trustworthy witnesses he was virtually put under oath and required to criminate himself. When solemnly appealed to by the high priest, he not only avowed his Messiahship, but asserted that he was the Son of God and the future judge of the world. He was then taken before Pontius Pilate, who gave the order for his death by crucifixion. He died in the act of commending his soul to God. The body was given by Pilate to Joseph* of Arimathea, and, aided by Nicodemus, he wrapped it in spices and laid it in a tomb prepared for himself in a garden which he owned outside the walls. Jesus rose on the third day after his death in the body, which, though changed as to its mode of being, was the identical body which was crucified. He was seen often in different places and circumstances by many witnesses. On the fortieth day after his resurrection, Jesus led the apostles out of Jerusalem towards Bethany and left them for the last time, not vanishing, as before, but passing visibly upward till a cloud concealed him from sight. While they looked after him two angels brought them a message—that he should "so come in like manner."

Christianity, the religion founded by Jesus Christ, may be regarded as divisible into—

(1) *Historical Christianity,* the facts and principles stated in the New Testament, especially those concerning the life, sufferings, death, resurrection, ascension and nature of Jesus, together with the subsequent development of the Christian Church, and the gradual embodiment in society of the principles inculcated in it.

(2) *Dogmatic Christianity,* the systems of theological doctrine founded on the New Testament. These systems differ with different churches, sects and schools.

(3) *Vital Christianity,* the Spirit manifested by Jesus Christ in his life, and which he commanded his followers to imitate.

———————————⊙———————————

The Crescent.

Mohammedanism Was Conceived in Abraham and Given Birth through Mohammed.

Abraham had only one son, Isaac, by his wife, Sarah, who was born in the year 1896 B. C. Four years after Isaac's birth, Ishmael, who was the son of Abraham by Sarah's Egyptian handmaid, Hagar, as is related in Genesis xxi., was driven into the wilderness with his mother. "And he will be a wild man; his hand will be against every man, and every man's hand against him; and he shall dwell in the presence of all his brethren" (Gen. xvi.). "Ishmael was blessed," and had twelve sons that became "princes according to their nations. And they dwelt from Havelah to Shur, that is before Egypt as thou goest towards Assyria" (Gen. xxv.). "They had golden earrings, because they were Ishmaelites"* (Judg. viii. 24). Ishmael died in the year 1773 B. C., "in the presence of all his brethren, at the age of 137 years." The Arabs regard him as their immediate ancestor.

The legend of the people is as follows: When our first parents were driven out of Paradise, they wandered until they finally settled on the border of the great Arabian desert. Here they built a temple, the Kaaba, in exact imitation of that in which they had worshiped in the Garden of Eden. Ten generations later a flood swept that region and destroyed the frail building, so that no vestige remained. Ten generations later, in a fit of cruel jealousy, Sarah, the wife of the patriarch Abraham, caused him to drive out his handmaid, Hagar,

and their son, Ishmael, and while wandering in the
desert an angel revealed this site to Hagar, and
she gave her thirsty son to drink of the refreshing
waters of its well Zem-Zem. It was here, on account of its goodly supply of water, the chief attraction in locating an Oriental city, that a tribe of
Amalekites came and founded the city of Mecca.
They aided Ishmael in rebuilding the Kaaba, and to
their assistance came the angel Gabriel, with a white
stone from Paradise, which even to-day is to be
found in the wall of the Kaaba, turned black by the
devout kisses of sinful lips.

In the sixth century of the present era the keeper
of this sacred stone was one Abdallah, a very poor
but noble man, of the tribe of Koreish, one of the
most distinguished Arabian tribes; the guardian-
ship of the Kaaba was hereditarily entrusted to it.
But his family, Hashem, was poor. Abdallah died
just before his first son was born. That son was
called Mohammed, "The Praised," and was born
in Mecca in the year 570. In later years, when
comparative deification of the prophet took place,
there were added to the circumstances of his birth,
legends similar to those of the other founders of
great religions. It is said that as soon as he was
born, he turned his eyes to the light and distinctly
said, "God is great and I am his prophet," the
river Tigris overflowed its banks, the palace of
King Chosroes toppled to the ground, the holy fires
of Zoroaster that had burned for centuries were
extinguished by the brighter light, and mules talked
and sheep bowed to him when he went out. He lost
his mother, Amena, when he was six years old, and

was adopted a few years later by his uncle, Abu-Taleb, with whom he went to Syria; there he met an Arab monk, who informed his uncle of the future awaiting his nephew, and charged him to guard the boy with the greatest care. From that time

THE PROPHET MOHAMMED.

until his twentieth year he is scarcely heard of. In that year he served in the war against the Beni Kinanah tribe. In his twenty-fifth year he was a shepherd on the pasture-fields in the vicinity of Mecca. About this time he entered the employ of a wealthy widow, who was some fifteen years his senior. This widow, Kadijah, employed him to look after her caravans, and his management of her affairs was attended with uniform success. On his return from a journey to Damascus, where he had met with greater success than ever, the exultant widow offered to marry him and pleaded her cause with such fervor and eloquence that the young man consented. In many respects this marriage was most important in its results. It at once placed Mohammed in a position of affluence and raised his rank equal to that of the influential tribe of the Koreish. Mohammed now gave up business and devoted himself to religious meditations. The religion of the Arabs at this time (595) was Sabaism, a kind of idolatry or system of sun, moon and star worship, widely prevalent, not only in Arabia, but in Chaldea, Syria and Ethiopia. Idolatry had overclouded the old Monotheism (one God) of the Arabs, and brought the religious instincts of the people into manifold confusion. Mohammed was surrounded by Jews, Christians and Jewish Christians; and in his journeys with the caravans had frequent opportunities of discussing religious questions with them. It is certain that he was far from satisfied with Judaism, Christianity or Sabaism, the popular religions of Arabia. The scenes of misery and immorality, and the utter spiritual degradation of the entire people, made a vivid impression on his sensitive mind, and suggested that remedies should be found.

In his fortieth year he received the first revelation concerning the new truth. He hastened to his beloved wife, and, confiding to her what had happened, fell into a severe paroxysm of epilepsy. He became subject to the most fearful mental torments. Hesitation and fear possessed him. In the end he overcame them, with the result that he felt himself called upon to overthrow the worship of his countrymen, establish the belief in the unity of God, and that he was the one divinely appointed to preach it to the world. The evidence of trustworthy historians goes to show that he was known for his kindness and gentleness, his honesty and truth, qualities that gained for him the surname of Al-Amin, "The True." His progress was slow, his footsteps were dogged, his foes persecuted him, his faithful wife, Kadijah, dies, and once he was stoned and left for dead by the roadside. At this juncture help came from an unexpected quarter. The neighboring city of Medina was held by two tribes hostile to the people of Mecca, and they offered him and his converts asylum. At the dead of night and at the peril of his life he fled from his birthplace, and that day is celebrated in the Mohammedan calendar as the beginning of a new era. This took place in the year 622, and is called the *Hegira*. His flight became known and pursuers followed him. He hid in a cave three days and nights. Tradition loves to tell how a spider wove its web over the cave's mouth, and some doves, ever after sacred, laid their eggs before the cave, so that the pursuers judged therefrom that none had entered the cave. Arrived at Medina, he organized his followers. From that time a complete change came over him; the man who had been "as shy as a veiled virgin," now became the apostle of war. With a small army of followers he overran Arabia, and in less than seven years his gleaming

sword had conquered every city of the land. Even
Mecca fell before him, and he threw out the idols
from the temple and consecrated it to the worship
of Allah. Acknowledged was he now by the whole
people as the prophet of God and as their king.

His great gift is the Mohammedan Bible, the
Koran, a book containing the messages of the
prophet which were collected by his follower, Zeid,
from records written on palm leaves, white stones,
leather, the shoulder-blades of sheep and camels.

Mohammedanism, the religion founded by Mohammed, or Mahomet, teaches, in opposition to the
various idolatrous religions which it has succeeded
in superseding, a strong theism (belief in God),
essentially the same as taught by Judaism and
Christianity, from which it was borrowed. "There
is no God but God" is the principal tenet in Mohammedan dogmatics, and he has created the world
and the immortal soul of man, whose life on earth
he shall judge and reward or punish in a future
state. But the further development of this idea,
especially of the relation between God and mankind, is narrow, fantastic and arbitrary. Before
the almighty power of Allah the free will of man
vanishes; Mohammedanism is fatalism. The Koran acknowledges and encourages polygamy, and
it exists in all Mohammedan countries, with all its
deteriorating and weakening consequences, spiritual and bodily.

Ten years after Mohammed had fled from Mecca,
in the year 632, at the age of sixty-two, he made a
pilgrimage thither from Medina with forty thousand Moslems, and there on a mountain, like Moses
of old, he uttered the last words to the people, ex-

horting them chiefly to protect the weak, the poor, the women, and to abstain from usury. He was sick for some days, the result of a poison administered to him by a woman. As he lay dying, with his head resting on the lap of Ayesha, one of the numerous wives he had wedded after the death of Kadijah, she heard him murmuring, as she looked into his pale face and slowly glazing eyes, "No . . . . . . the companions above . . . . . . in Paradise." She took his hand in hers, praying. When she let it sink it was cold, and he was dead. He left ten wives (of fourteen, which he had in all), but only one child, Fatima, the daughter of Kadijah, his first wife; and so long as Kadijah lived, Mohammed did not follow the practice usual among Arabs of taking many wives. He was buried in the mosque at Medina, and at his tomb thousands of pilgrims gather every year.

Islam is the Arabic name for the Mohammedan creed. Moslem is the name the professors of this creed give themselves. Saracens or Mussulmans, followers of Mohammed.

———————————

The Conflict.

Mutual hatred had long existed between the Christians and the Mohammedans. The latter aforetime had done incalculable damage to the prospects of the Cross. All that the missionaries and evangelists had accomplished in Arabia, Abyssinia, Egypt and northern Africa, had been eradicated by the followers of the prophet. The movement of the Mohammedans, westward through Africa and northward into Europe, in the eighth century, was answered by the counter movement of the Christians, eastward through Europe and into Asia, in the eleventh. The sword of the living Godfrey was crossed with that of the dead Taric.

Previous to the opening of the conflict, however, and indirectly leading to it, Palestine had become the Mecca of pious pilgrims, who, from all parts of Christendom, threaded their weary way to the land made sacred by their Lord and Master, that they might do penance for their sins or quicken their zeal by visiting hallowed scenes. A great stimulus was given to these undertakings by the mother of Constantine, Helena, who visited the Holy Land in A. D. 325, and in pious zeal used the immense wealth at her command in building altars, chapels and houses of prayer in places made historical by events in the Saviour's life. She erected the famous Church of the Nativity at Bethlehem, the city of His birth; built the Church of the Holy Sepulchre at Jerusalem, on the supposed site of His tomb; and laid the foundations of the Church of the Resurrection. Her industrious example naturally awakened new zeal for pilgrimage. Henceforth, thousands upon thousands, princes and peasants, nobles and beggars, the devout and the mercenary, annually thronged the thoroughfares on their way to the "City of the Great King."

But while this was going on, Jerusalem, then under the control of the Roman Empire, was taken possession of in 637, by the soldiers of Islam, commanded by that famous Mohammedan chieftain, Omar. He erected the mosque bearing his name, on the site of the temple of Solomon, and restored the enclosures of the temple—a tribute paid to King Solomon, whose faith, like Mohammed's, recognized but one "Living and True God." Owing to Omar's tolerance, for a long period the Christians were undisturbed in their pilgrimages and devotions, but in 1073 Palestine was overrun and conquered by hordes of Seljook* Turks, who came out of the northeast through Khorassan and other provinces of Persia. They were more in the form of revolutionists than conquerors, as they were already the disciples of Islam. The Arabian Fatimite* governors were obliged to retire into Egypt. The Holy City fell under the dominion of Sultan Malek Shah and his viceroys, who instituted a high revel of violence and outrage against both Christians and Arabs. Infested by bands of lawless men, the roads to Jerusalem became no longer safe for pilgrims. They were robbed of their much or little wealth; men were thrown into slavery; women were outraged; children were stolen or murdered, and although, doubtless, there were enthusiasts who courted these perils in the holy cause, yet the vast majority of Christendom were filled with grief and vengeance as returning pilgrims told the ghastly tale of pagan atrocities.

In this state of affairs, when there was scarcely a home circle that was not saddened or bereaved by the brutal treatment of the pilgrims, Peter the Hermit, a monk and native of Amiens in France, having visited Palestine and witnessed the cruelty of the Turks, reported what he had seen to Pope Urban II., by whom encouraged, he traveled through Italy and France and began to preach the first Crusade. Peter had been educated in Paris and in Italy; had served in the army of Flanders, but gave up the military career and married; became a monk after the death of his wife, and finally a hermit. Possessed of no other power than the influence of his character and his genius, this simple unshod monk, a man of mean aspect, clad in a coarse cassock, around which a rude rope served as a girdle, mounted on a mule, and holding a gleaming crucifix in his hand, rode from town to town and from province to province rehearsing the indignities heaped upon the innocent pilgrims; in graphic language he depicted the scenes of blood of which he had been an eye-witness in the streets of Jerusalem, appealing in turn to the piety, the courage and the passions of his hearers. By his eloquence he fired the popular heart to go forth to redress the wrongs and rescue a desecrated tomb from the hands of the infidel. As a consequence

of his impassioned harangues, such a wave of enthusiasm for his enterprise surged throughout

PREACHING THE CRUSADE

Christendom that the reigning powers felt its
mighty swell, and in the year 1095, at the Council

of Clermont, Pope Urban II. espoused his cause and gave pontifical sanction to the first Crusade. Previous to the setting out of the *true* Crusade, four armies, if they may be so named, consisting of disorderly multitudes of the dregs of Christendom, had departed for Palestine.

The eastern frontiers of France became the scene of the gathering. There Peter the Hermit, as the chief promoter of the enterprise, assumed the leadership of the host. Without adequate preparation, without suitable arms, without any appreciation of the dangers and difficulties to be encountered, the vast and tumultuous throng swept out of France and into Germany. The great sea of angry and excited humanity overflowed the ordinary routes of travel, and spread devastation on every hand. The means of subsistence were quickly exhausted, and the multitudes began to prey on the countries through which they traversed. They swept on through the German territories like an army of devouring locusts, until through sheer waste of resources they were obliged to divide into smaller masses. One band, numbering about 20,000, commanded by Walter the Penniless, a French knight, of Burgundy, pressed forward through Hungary and Bulgaria in the direction of Constantinople. The Bulgarians took up arms to defend their country from destruction. The track of Walter and his army was marked with blood and fire. The Crusaders were cut off day by day until, at the confines of the country, only Walter and a few followers remained to make their way through the forests to Constantinople.

Meanwhile the second division of the host, numbering about 40,000 men, women and children, under the command of Peter the Hermit, pressed on in the same direction taken by Walter. They, too, were pursued and furiously attacked by the wild Bulgarians, who caused a general rout and slaughter of thousands of their number. The remaining wretched, half-starved fugitives in time arrived at Constantinople, where, under the protection of Emperor Alexius, who had espoused the Crusade, the two united their forces, crossed the Bosphorus into Asia Minor, and encountered the Turks at Nice. There they were utterly routed and slaughtered; Walter the Penniless was killed and the remaining remnant returned to Constantinople. A third rabble soon followed from Germany. A certain monk named Godeschal, envious of the fame of Peter and Walter, preached the holy war through his native districts, and about 15,000 villagers and peasants flocked to his standard. They followed the same route as the others, and before the walls of Belgrade they were massacred by the Hungarians, almost to a man.

In the meantime, the fourth and last division of the host gathered on the eastern confines of Germany. Perhaps no other such a detestable mass of vile humanity was seen before or since in the world. France sent her thieves; the Rhine provinces, their offscouring; the British Islands, their outlaws; and all the west, her pads and murderers. This delightful army of European refuse heaped up to the number of more than 200,000. A few ignorant nobles with their bands of retainers were merged in the common mass; but when it came to the election of leaders the choice fell on *a goat and*

a goose. These ridiculous creatures were actually
set forward as the divinely constituted agents by
which the host was to be led to victory over the
infidel Turks of Asia. The result was as revolting
as the beginning was abominable. The superstitious
herd fell upon the Jewish colonists in the cities of
the Rhine and the Moselle, and began to rob and
murder. The rabble pretended to see in the Jews
only the enemies of Christ. In spite of the protests
of the Romish Church, under whose call the Crusade
had been begun, the Jews were massacred by thousands. When the ruffian hosts could find no further
material to slaughter, the march was resumed from
the Rhine to the Danube. The whole route was a
scene of barbarous lust and licentiousness. The day
of judgment, however, at last arrived. At the Danube the Hungarian army was drawn up to dispute
the progress of the invaders. The immense rabble
was hemmed in and beaten back against the river.
The tide of the Danube was red with the blood of the
robbers. Very few escaped the vengeance of the
Hungarians and the engulfing river. Thus perished
the fourth and last of those fanatic multitudes that
arose at the call of Peter the Hermit. Already
more than a quarter of a million of human beings
had been swallowed from sight before a regular
army could be equipped and started in the wake
of the popular tumult. Not a Christian soldier
had thus far penetrated beyond the plain of Nice.
Walter the Penniless was dead. The fame of Peter
the Hermit was also at a discount, but the fever
of Europe was in nowise cooled. It still remained
for her soldiery to undertake by regular expedition

what her peasants and monks, her goose and her goat, had failed to accomplish.

In the meantime the secular princes of the west, who attended the Council of Clermont and assumed the Cross, were busily engaged in preparing for the holy war. A vast army embracing all the chivalry of Europe, consisting of six grand divisions, set forth for Constantinople. Here they united their forces and then took up their march for the Holy City. Among those who were destined to distinguish themselves as Crusaders, should be mentioned, first of all, Godfrey of Bouillon, Duke of Lorraine. His reputation for piety, learning and courage was equal to that of the best prince of his age. In his father's house Peter the Hermit had lived before he became a monk. In early life Godfrey took up arms and won high distinction as a soldier in many bloody fought battles. With no half-hearted purpose did he become a Crusader. No sacrifices were spared to secure the desired end. He sold or mortgaged all of his castles and estates, and with the money procured by the sale of his vast domains he raised and equipped a magnificent army of 90,000 men. It was he who led those from Germany and northern France.

Raymond, Count of Toulouse, a second of the leaders, was a soldier by profession and had fought against the Mohammedans in Spain. He was known as one of the most valiant captains of his times. It was his saying that he had spent his youth fighting the followers of the false prophet in Europe, and would spend his old age in warring with them in Asia. Already aged, his white locks made him a conspicuous leader for those from southern France.

Prince Bohemond, of Tarentum, Italy, who led the Italian force, was the tallest man in his army; he was full of passion and haughty pride; when he spoke, his hearers believed that eloquence had been his only study; when under arms, he might be supposed to have done nothing but wield the lance and sword. The deliverance of the tomb of Christ was not the object that induced him to assume the Cross; he hoped to win a kingdom before he should arrive at Jerusalem. After the fall of Antioch* his vain hopes were realized by his becoming the first Prince of Antioch.

Hugh the Great, Count of Vermandois, led the French forces. He was a brother of King Philip of France. At home he was much admired for his brilliant qualities by the Court. He was brave, but easily overcome by flattery, and was wanting in perseverance in reverses.

Robert, Duke of Normandy, who led the Norman forces, was the son of William the Conqueror. He had few noble qualities, but many reprehensible faults. His extravagance, weakness and inconstancy caused him to be unpopular, and, in the end, reduced him to absolute poverty.

Robert, Count of Flanders, was at the head of the Frisons and the Flemings, or Dutch forces. He embarked in an expedition which procured for him the reputation of a bold knight, together with the surname of "The Lance and Sword" of the Christians.

All these leaders were celebrated for their exploits, but no one amongst that vast army was more worthy to attract the attention of posterity than the brave Tancred, from the island of Sicily, whose piety and friendship for his cousin, Prince Bohemond, under whom he served, led him into Asia. A stranger to all the motives and interests of policy, he acknowledged no other law but religion and honor, and was always ready to die in their cause.

THE FIRST CRUSADE.

He was made Prince of Tiberias, and finally died at Antioch in 1112.

The forces thus gathered out of the prolific west numbered fully 600,000 warriors. Of these, 100,-000 were mounted knights, and the remainder, foot soldiers in armor. The mixed character of the throng was still preserved. Priest, matron and maid journeyed by the side of the warriors. At the head rode the austere Godfrey, the white-haired

Raymond, and Peter the Hermit seated on a mule. This immense army pressed steadily forward, and after capturing Nice, Antioch and other cities on the way, this army, though greatly reduced in numbers by privations and conflict, at length came upon the object of its ambition, Jerusalem, in the year 1099. The city was taken on the 15th of July, after an obstinate siege of somewhat more than five weeks. Assault after assault was made upon the unyielding walls, only to be repulsed, and the jaded remnant of only 40,000 of what was once a vast army, were on the point of abandoning the undertaking, when Godfrey, looking up to Mount Olivet, beheld there a mighty horseman waving on high a buckler. "Behold," cried the hero, "St. George comes again to our aid and makes a signal for us to enter the Holy City." The effect was magical. The army, seized as if by an electric enthusiasm, made an irresistible charge, carried the walls, and Jerusalem was taken. History has remarked that the Christians entered Jerusalem on a Friday, at the hour of three in the afternoon; exactly the same day and hour at which Christ expired for the salvation of the human race. Among those who received the greatest congratulations by the victorious multitude was Peter the Hermit. The little fanatic monk was singled out as the greatest of all the human agencies by which the deliverance of Jerusalem had been accomplished. Around him, clad in his woolen garment and mounted on his mule, the mediæval Zealots gathered in enormous crowds, and did obeisance as to a liberator and savior. Godfrey of Bouillon soon came in for his share of glory. Within eight days after the fall of the city he was on the 23d of July elected king of Jerusalem. Godfrey accepted the office, but refused the title of king. He declared that it would be unbecoming in him to wear a crown of gold in the city where Christ had been crowned with thorns. It was therefore decided that he be entitled "First

. JERUSALEM.

Baron and Defender of the Holy Sepulchre." His sovereignty, however, was ample and his right undisputed. Soon after many of the princes and leaders returned to Europe. Peter the Hermit likewise left the Holy City and started on a homeward voyage. In mid-sea his ship was caught in a storm and the terrified monk vowed if he should be spared

he would found an abbey in honor of the tomb of
Christ. The tempest passed and Peter kept his vow
by building a monastery on the banks of the Maes
in France. Here he spent the remnant of his days
in penitential works, after the manner of his order.

About a year after the taking of Jerusalem, as
Godfrey was returning from an expedition, the
emir of Cæsarea* came out to meet him and
presented to him an offering of some of the fruits
of Palestine. The unsuspecting Godfrey accepted
and ate an apple. Doubtless it had been poisoned,
for the prince almost immediately fell ill. It was
with great difficulty that he reached Jaffa, whence
he was conveyed to his capital, where on the 18th of
July, 1100, he died. His mortal remains were deposited within the enclosure of Calvary, near the
tomb of Christ. He surpassed all the captains of
his age, and his name will live honored amongst
men as long as the remembrance of the Crusades.
Godfrey was succeeded by his brother Baldwin of
Edessa, as Baldwin I., and upon his death in 1118,
was succeeded by Baldwin de Bourg, a cousin of
Baldwin I., under the title of Baldwin II.

Ancient Templars.

The conquest of the city furnished a new stimulus to the pilgrim age, but Palestine was still in the
hands of the fierce Mohammedans, who soon began
to carry on their work of pillage and murder of
Christian pilgrims with increased vigor. In 1118
two French knights, Hugh de Payens and Geoffrey
of Saint Omar, perceiving the hardships to which
the Christian travelers were exposed in and about

the Holy City, took upon themselves the duty of conducting the pilgrims who journeyed between Jerusalem and the Jordan. This charitable office soon gained reputation for the humble warrior guides, and they were joined by seven others, like-minded with themselves. Their names were Royal, Gundemar, Godfrey Bisol, Payens de Montidur, Archibald de St. Aman, Andre de St. Moulbar, and the Count of Province. An organization was effected under the benevolent patronage of the patriarch of the city, and under the name of "Poor Fellow Soldiers of Christ." The members bound themselves by the usual monastic vow of obedience, chastity and poverty; and to these two others were added, to defend the Holy Sepulchre and to protect the wayfaring pilgrims in Palestine. Such was the humble beginning of the Order of Knights Templar. At this time I deem it best to mention that the old established Order of Knights Hospitallers, who were now in the flush of their heroic victories, lent aid and encouragement to the new society of brothers. Nothing was to be feared by the Knights Hospitallers from an humble fraternity known by the name of "Poor Fellow-soldiers of Christ," but in years afterwards jealousy arose, and sometimes conflict between the two orders, yet for the most part they fought side by side for the common cause.

Hugh and Geoffrey had but one horse between them, and him they rode together on their first mission of benevolence. (The great seal of the Templars still perpetuates the story of the lowly origin of the Order in the figure of a steed with two riders.) The first members were given a lodging by

Baldwin II., who assigned them quarters in his palace on the site of the ancient temple, whence they derived the name of Templars; a title which they ever afterward retained.

Their first armory was established in a church near by, and here they stored their knightly weapons. The first Chapter was limited to nine members; but this limitation was removed by the Council of Troyes in 1127. Raynouard says that Baldwin sent Hugh de Payens to Europe to solicit a new Crusade, and that while there he presented his companions to the Pope Honorius II., from whom he craved permission to form a religious military order, in imitation of that of the Hospitallers. The Pontiff referred them to the ecclesiastical council which was then in session at Troyes, in Champagne. Thither De Payens repaired, and represented to the fathers the vocation of himself and his companions as defenders of the pilgrim; the enterprise was approved, and St. Bernard, Abbot of Clairvaux, was commissioned to draw up a suitable code for the government of the body, and to devise an appropriate garb. The dress chosen was in strong contrast with that of the Knights Hospitallers, consisting of a white tunic and mantle, with a red cross on the left breast, while the Knights Hospitallers wore the plain black robe, bearing a white cross of eight points on the left breast. The rule of conduct and discipline was approved in 1128 by Pope Honorius II. The principal articles were these: The Knights were bound to recite vocal prayers at certain hours; to abstain from meats four days in the week; to refrain from hunting and hawking; to defend with their lives the mysteries of the Christian

faith; to observe and maintain the seven sacraments
of the church, the fourteen articles of faith, the
creeds of the apostles and of Athanasius;* to up-
hold the doctrines of the two Testaments, including
the interpretations of the Fathers, the unity of God
and the trinity of his person, and the virginity of
Mary both before and after the birth of the Son;
to go beyond the seas when called to do so in defense
of the cause; to fly not from the foe unless assailed
by more than three infidels at once. Hugh de Payens, thus provided with a rule that gave perma-
nence to his Order, and encouraged by the approval
of the church, returned to Jerusalem. Humility
was one of the first principles of the membership.
The helmet of the Templar should have no crest—
his beard should not be cut—his demeanor should be
that of servant of his fellows. Each member, on
assuming the garb of a Knight, must be girt with
a linen cord in token that he was henceforth bound
to service.

The primal object sought in the institution of
the Order was the succor of needy pilgrims; but as
the Moslems recovered after the capture of Jerusalem, and in increasing numbers threatened the
Christians on every side, the organization from necessity assumed a more distinctively military character, and ultimately became the right arm of the
Christian armies in their several operations against
the foe. St. Bernard, who visited them in their
Temple retreat, speaks in the warmest terms of
their self-denial, their frugality, their modesty,
their piety, and their bravery. Their banner was
the Beauseant, of divided white and black, indi-

cative of peace to their friends, but destruction to their foes.

The organization of the Templars embraced four classes of members—Knights, Squires, Servitors and Priests. Each had their peculiar duties and obligations. The presiding officer of the Order was called the Master—afterwards the Grand Master. England, Germany, France and Italy, in fact, nearly all the states of Christendom, were divided into provinces, and over each was set a provincial Master. The Grand Master of Jerusalem was regarded as the head of the entire brotherhood, which soon grew in numbers, influence and wealth to be one of the most powerful organizations in the world. Counts, dukes, princes, and even kings, eagerly sought the honor which was everywhere conceded to the red cross and white mantle of the Templar.

In course of time the Knights of the Temple became a sovereign body, owing no allegiance to any secular potentate. In spiritual matters the Pope was still regarded as supreme, but in all other affairs the Grand Master was as independent as the greatest sovereign of Europe. The houses of the Knights could not be invaded by any civil officer. Their churches and cemeteries were exempt from interdicts; their properties and revenues from taxation. So great were the immunities thus enjoyed that thousands of persons sought to be affiliated with the brotherhood in order to share its benefits.

To the Knights Templar and the Hospitallers was largely due whatever success or glory the subsequent Crusades achieved, of which there were seven. They were the flower of the armies, always in the van with their glittering swords and waving banners, when duty called; and whether defending moated castle, or mountain defiles, they fought with that dauntless heroism which makes even the sword almost an object of reverence. When the Christian kingdom in the East tottered to its downfall, the Templars attempted to secure their own interests by separate treaties with the Moslems, but their fortunes were involved with those of the Western powers, and all went down together. The chief seat of the Templars remained at Jerusalem from the foundation in 1118 until 1187, when Saladin, Sultan of Egypt, invaded Palestine, and in October of that year captured Jerusalem; it was then transferred to Antioch, which fell to the Christians in 1098, during the first Crusade. It was there that the followers of Christ first took the name of Christians; it was there that St. Peter was made first bishop of the church; and there the early saints and martyrs performed their miracles that gave to the city a sanctity second only to that of Jerusalem. The headquarters of the Grand Master remained at Antioch for four years, and was then removed in 1191 to Acre.* This city was first taken by Baldwin I. in 1100, recaptured by the Moslems under Saladin in 1187, and again retaken in 1191, by Richard Coeur de Lion, leader of the third Crusade. It was estimated that at this siege the Christian losses reached the enormous aggregate of three hundred thousand men, while those of the Moslems were but little inferior. In all the great struggles of human history so terrible a waste of life was never witnessed as before the walls of Acre. It became the stronghold of Knighthood and continued to be the headquarters of the Order until 1217,

when a third removal was made to the Pilgrims
Castle near Cæsarea, a city founded by Herod the
Great, in 22 B. C., and built in honor of Cæsar.
It was situated northwest of Jerusalem on the Mediterranean, and north of Jaffa, but now lies in shapeless ruins. In 1291 the city of Acre again fell into
the hands of the Moslems under Sultan Khatil of
Cairo, and with the subsequent overthrow of the
Christian kingdom, the Templars retired to the
island of Cyprus, which was captured in 1191 by
Richard Cœur de Lion, during the third Crusade,
and to whom they paid thirty-five thousand marks.
Many of the Templars, after a brief stay in the
island of Cyprus, retired to their different Preceptories in Europe. A brief description of the defense
and fall of Acre can only be compared with the
many accounts of their past glorious struggles with
the infidel in defense of the Holy Land, and of Christian pilgrimage, sometimes successful and often dis-
astrous; of arid sands well moistened with the blood
of Christian and Saracen warriors; of final forced
departure from the places which its prowess had
conquered, but which it had not the strength to
hold.

Defense and Fall of Acre.

With less than twelve thousand persons able to
bear arms, they manned the ramparts and defended
the city against two hundred thousand Moslems.
Almost every nation of Europe was represented
in the multitudes that thronged the streets that had
gathered within the defenses of the city. On the
fourth of May, a day fatal to the Christians,

BATTLE BEFORE ACRE.

the signal for the last assault was given. At dawn
the Moslem army was under arms, the Sultan ani-

147

mating the soldiers by his presence. Both the attack and defense were much greater than the days before. Among those who fell on the field of battle, there were seven Moslems for one Christian; but the Moslems could repair their losses; those of the Christians were irreparable. With ever-increasing vehemence the Moslems leveled their destroying engines against the tottering walls and towers of the city. At last an important defense, known by the name of the Cursed Tower, yielded to the assailants, and went down with a crash. The breach thus effected in the defenses opened into the heart of the city. The Templars formed a rash resolution of making a sortie, and attacking the camp of the Moslems; they found the enemies drawn up in order of battle. After a bloody conflict the Templars were repulsed and pursued to the foot of the ramparts. The Grand Master of the Templars, William de Beaujeu, one of the bravest of the brave, was struck by an arrow and fell in the midst of his Knights. The Grand Master of the Hospitallers at the same time received a wound which disabled him. The rout then became general, and all hope of saving the city was lost. In poured the savage tides of victorious Islam, hungry for blood and revenge. It was then a death-pall seemed stretched over the whole city of Acre; there was not a street that did not become the theater of carnage; a battle was fought for every tower, for every palace, and at the entrance of every public building; and in all these combats so many men were killed, that, according to the report of an historian, "they walked upon the dead as upon a bridge." A violent storm, accompanied by hail and rain, burst over the city;

the horizon was all at once covered with such impenetrable darkness that the combatants could scarcely distinguish the colors they fought under, or see the standards floated over the towers; the flames appeared in several quarters without any one making an effort to extinguish them; the conquerors only thought of destroying the city; the only object of the conquered was to escape. Whole families took refuge in churches, where they were stifled by the flames, or cut to pieces at the foot of the altars; many women and timid virgins, to preserve their chastity, cut off their noses and otherwise disfigured themselves to escape the brutality of the conquerors, for when the Moslems beheld their bleeding faces, they would conceive a disgust for them and put them to the sword at once.

The castle of the Templars, situated on the sea-coast, in which all the Knights had taken refuge who had escaped the steel of the Moslems, was the only place in the city that had held out. After several days' siege, the Sultan granted a capitulation, and sent three hundred Moslems to execute the treaty. Scarcely had these entered one of the principal towers, the tower of the Grand Master, than they began to outrage the women who had taken refuge there. This violation of the rights of war irritated the Christian warriors to such a degree that all the Moslems who entered the tower were put to death. The angry Sultan ordered the siege renewed at once, and that all Templars in the asylum be put to the sword. The Templars and their companions defended themselves for several days; at length the tower of the Grand Master was undermined, and fell at the very moment the Moslems were mounting to an assault. They who attacked it and they who defended it were equally crushed by its fall; women, children, Christian warriors, all who had come to seek refuge in the house of the Templars, perished, buried beneath the ruins. Such was the dash, bravery and self-sacrifice of the Templars throughout the life of the Order. To follow their acts of true heroism would be to give a history of the Crusades.

The few Christians still clinging to the coast town of Syria made their escape as soon as possible and left the savage Moslems in complete possession of the country. After a continuance of 191 years, the contest between the Cross and the Crescent had ended in a complete restoration of the ancient régime throughout Syria and Asia Minor. The Crescent of Islam was again in the ascendant.

Final Dissolution.

In the beginning of the fourteenth century, Philip the Fair, an avaricious and ambitious king of France, secretly planned with Pope Clement V. for the destruction of the Templars and the appropriation of their revenue. The Order at this time was enormously wealthy; this aroused his avarice. Their power interfered with his designs of political aggrandizement and this alarmed his ambition. Pope Clement, by Philip's direction, wrote, in 1306, to De Molay, the Grand Master, who was then at Cyprus, inviting him to come and consult with him on some matters of great importance to the Order. De Molay obeyed the summons and arrived at Paris with sixty Knights and a large amount of treasure.

He was arrested and imprisoned, as was later every Knight in France, on the pretended charge of idolatry, and other enormous crimes, of which a renegade and expelled prior of the Order was said to have confessed that the Knights were guilty of in

BURNING OF JAQUES DE MOLAY.

their Chapters. On such preposterous charges the Knights were tried, and, of course, as a foregone conclusion, condemned, and on the 12th of May, 1310, fifty-four of the Knights were publicly burned. De Molay, during his imprisonment, was subjected to the utmost indignities and sufferings for the purpose of extorting from him a confession of the guilt of his Order. But De Molay was firm and loyal, and on the 11th day of March, 1314, he was publicly burned "in the little island" of the Seine between the "Augustinians and the royal garden" in Paris. When about to die he solemnly affirmed the innocence of the Order, and it is said summoned Pope Clement to appear before the judgment-seat of God in forty days and the king of France within a year, and both, it is well known, died within the periods specified. In most countries their property was seized by the sovereign and in part turned over to the Hospitallers and other Orders. From the establishment of the Order by Hugh de Payens, the first Grand Master, in 1118, until its dissolution (1311) during the Mastership of James De Molay, twenty-two Grand Masters presided over the Order.

Knights Templar, Masonic.

The connection of the Knights Templar with the Freemasons may much more plausibly be traced than that of the Knights of Malta. Yet, unfortunately, the sources from which information is to be derived are for the most part traditionary; authentic dates and documents are wanting.

There are four sources from which Masonic Templars are said to have derived their existence, making therefore as many different divisions of the Order.

1. The Templars who claim John Mark Larmenius as the successor of De Molay. From this source came the Templars of France.

2. Those who recognize Peter d'Aumont as the successor of De Molay. From this source came the Templars of Germany.

3. Those who derive their Templarism from the Count Beaujeu, the nephew of De Molay. From this source came the Swedish Templars.

4.   Those who claim an independent origin, and repudiate alike the authority of Larmenius, of Aumont and of Beaujeu.

Of the last class, or the Templars who recognized the authority of neither of the leaders who have been mentioned, there were two subdivisions, the Scotch and the English; for it is only in Scotland and England that this independent Templarism found a foothold.

The English Masonic Templars are most probably derived from that body called the "Baldwyn Encampment" of Bristol, or from some one of the co-ordinate Encampments of London, Bath, York and Salisbury, which it is claimed were formed by the members of the Preceptory,[1] which had long existed at Bristol, and who, on the dissolution of their Order, are supposed to have united with the Masonic fraternity. The Baldwyn Encampment claims to have existed from "time immemorial"—an indefinite period—but we can trace it back far enough to give it a priority over all other English Encampments.[2] From this division of the Templars, repudiating all connections with Larmenius, with Aumont, or any other of the self-constituted leaders, but tracing its origin to the independent action of Knights who fled for security and for perpetuity into the body of Masonry, are we, I think, says Dr. Mackey, justly entitled to derive the Templars of the United States. Just at what time Commanderies were organized in this country, there is no

---

[1] See Commandery, page 111, third and fourth paragraphs.
[2] See Baldwyn Encampment, in Supplement.

definite date. Boston Commandery claims to date from 1769, and is supposed to be one of the oldest.

Such in outline is the illustrous military history of the Order of Knights Templar. The outward may pass away; the torn banners, the gleaming shield, the burnished armor, the quivering blades, together with the forms that bore them so gallantly, may become dust, or at best preserved in history and song, but the knightly spirit may ever abide in true men and be exemplified in every age.

Knights of Malta.

This Order, which at various times in the progress of its history, received the names of Knights Hospitallers, Knights of St. John of Jerusalem, Knights of Rhodes, and lastly, Knights of Malta, was the oldest and one of the most important of the religious and military orders of Knighthood which sprang into existence during the Crusades, which were instituted for the recovery of the Holy Land. It owes its origin to the Hospitallers of Jerusalem, that wholly religious and charitable Order, which was established at Jerusalem in 1048 by some pious and benevolent merchants of the Italian city of Amalfi, for the succor of poor and distressed Latin pilgrims.

This society, established when Jerusalem was in the hands of Mohammedans, passed through many vicissitudes, but lived to see the Holy Land conquered by the Christian Knights. It then received many accessions from the Crusaders, who, laying aside their arms, devoted themselves to the pious avocation of attending the sick. It was then, in the year 1099, that Gerard, the Rector of the Hospital, induced the brethren to take upon themselves the vows of poverty, obedience and chastity. The habit selected for the Order was a plain black robe, bearing a white cross of eight points on the left breast.

Raymond de Puy succeeded Gerard and proposed a change in the character of the society, by which it should become a Military Order, devoted to active labors in the field and the protection of Palestine from the encroachment of the infidels. This proposition was warmly approved by Baldwyn, the king of Jerusalem, who, harassed by a continual warfare, gladly accepted this addition to his forces. The Order having thus been organized on a military basis, the members took a new oath, by which they bound themselves to defend the cause of Christianity, but on no account to bear arms for any other purpose. "This was in the same year that the ancient Order of Templars was organized and in the same city."

This act, done in 1118, is considered as the beginning of the establishment of the Order of Knights Hospitallers of St. John, of which Raymond DePuy is, by all historians, deemed the first Grand Master. They derived their title from the church and monastery built at Jerusalem in 1048 by the founders of the Order, and dedicated to St. John the Baptist. The history of the Knights from this time to the middle of the sixteenth century is but a chronicle of continued warfare with the enemies of the Christian faith. When Jerusalem was captured by Saladin in 1187, the Hospitallers retired to Margat, a town and fortress of Palestine which still acknowledged the Christian sway. At this epoch, the Hospitallers suffered much from their disputes and rivalries with the Templars; but in times of danger both brotherhoods gave their best blood in defense of the common cause. In 1191 they made Acre their principal place of residence, and in 1291, after the fall of that city, they fled to the island of Cyprus, where they established their convent. It was there they became a maritime power, having their own fleets and winning their own victories in the eastern Mediterranean. In time their residence in Cyprus became unpleasant. The king, by heavy taxes and other rigorous exactions, had so disgusted them, that early in the fourteenth century they left and seized the island of Rhodes, where they established their power and defied the Turks for more than two hundred years. In the latter part of 1522 they were attacked by the Turkish forces and surrendered. The Knights were permitted to retire with all their personal property, whence they sailed away and sought refuge in the island of Crete or Candia; from there to Messina in the island of Sicily, and then to the mainland of Italy, where, after seven years' negotiations with Emperor Charles V. of Germany, they obtained complete control of the island of Malta, and in 1530 they took formal possession. From this time the Order received the name of "Knights of Malta."

The sea-born possession they converted into a fortress which, in spite of the most strenuous efforts of the Turks, was held by the Knights until 1798, when it was surrendered without a struggle by Louis de Hompesch, the imbecile and pusillanimous Grand Master, to the French army and fleet under

Bonaparte; and this event may be considered as the commencement of the suppression of the Order as an active power. All that remains of it now is but the diluted shadow of its former existence. The Order, during its residence in Rhodes, underwent several changes in its organization, by which the simpler system observed during its infancy in the Holy Land was rendered more perfect and more complicated. In 1320 the Order was divided into eight languages, covering that number of provinces, over each of which presided one of the Grand dignataries with the title of Conventual Bailiff. Each of these dignitaries resided in the palace or inn, while the Hospitallers were at Rhodes and later at Malta, which was appropriated to his language. In every province there were one or more Grand Priories presided over by Grand Priors, and beneath these were the Commanderies, over each of which was a Commander. Now only the languages of Italy and Germany remain, and the functions of the Grand Master are exercised by a Lieutenant of the Magistery, who resides at Rome.

The Ancient Order of Malta has no connection with Masonry whatever, but was probably introduced by Thomas S. Webb as an appendant degree to the Order of the Temple, and in this country is conferred in the Asylum of a Commandery, or in a Priory regularly convened for that purpose.

THE END.

Supplemental Encyclopædia

OF

Ancient Countries and Cities

WITH

Short Sketches of the Early Tribes and of the Ancient
Characters Connected with Masonic History.

Supplemental Encyclopædia of Ancient Countries and Cities.

Aaron—The son of Amram and Jochebed, of the tribe of Levi, and brother of Moses and Miriam, born in the year 1574 B. C. He was three years older than Moses and apparently some years younger than their sister Miriam. Being an impulsive and eloquent man, he was appointed spokesman to Moses, whom he assisted in the deliverance of the Israelites from the bondage in Egypt. His wife was Elisheba, daughter of Aminadab, from whom he had four sons. Aaron's chief distinction consisted in the choice of him and his male posterity for the priesthood. He was consecrated the first high priest of the Israelites. He died on Mount Hor, in Edom, which is still called the "Mountain of Aaron," in the fortieth year after leaving Egypt, at the age of 123 years, and was succeeded in the priesthood by his son Eleazer. The Arabs still pretend to show his tomb on the mount, and highly venerate it.

Abraham or **Abram**—A son of Terah, a descendant of Shem, and born at Ur, in Mesopotamia, in 1996 B. C. In 1922 B. C. he went to Haran, in Mesopotamia, accompanied by his father, his wife Sarai, his brother Nahor, and his nephew Lot (Gen. xi. 26-32). His father dies soon after, and he takes Lot and his wife Sarai, and goes to Canaan. In 1920 B. C. they go to Egypt, but return in two years and Abram and Lot separate; Lot goes to Sodom and Abram to the Valley of Mamre; the same is Hebron in the land of Canaan. Sarai, being barren, gives Hagar, her Egyptian handmaid, to Abram, and in 1910 B. C. Ishmael was born. God covenants with Abram, changes his name to Abraham, institutes circumcision, and promises Isaac by Sarai, whom he calls Sarah (Gen. xvi., xvii.). In 1896 B. C. Isaac is born, and four years later Abraham sends Ishmael and Hagar away by request of Sarah. In 1859 B. C. Sarah dies, and Abraham, five years later, marries Keturah, by whom he had six sons. In 1821 B. C. Abraham dies at the age of 175 years, and is buried in the cave of Machpelah. Ishmael dies in 1773 B. C., at the age of 137 years.

In 1856 B. C. Isaac marries Rebekah, and in 1836 B. C. twin sons were born, whom they called Jacob and Esau (Gen. xxv.). Isaac dies at Hebron in 1716 B. C., aged 180 years, and is buried in the tomb of Abraham by his two sons (Gen. xxxv.).

In 1753 B. C. Jacob marries Leah and Rachel, and has six sons and one daughter by Leah: Reuben, Simeon, Levi, Judah, Isaachar, Zebulun and Dinah; two sons by Rachel's handmaid Bilhah: Dan and Naphtali; two by Zilpah, Leah's handmaid: Gad and Asher; two by Rachel: Joseph and Benjamin. In 1689 B. C. Jacob dies in Egypt, aged 147, and was buried in Canaan (Gen. l. 6-13).

Acre—A city of the tribe of Asher (Judg. i. 31). It was called by the Phœnicians, Accho; by the Greeks, Ptolemais, from one of the Ptolemies, who enlarged and beautified it. The Crusaders gave it the name of Acre, or St. John of Acre. It is called Akka by the Turks. It is a city and seaport of Syria, and is on the Mediterranean, thirty miles south of Tyre. It was the "Key to Palestine," and has been the scene of many famous sieges and battles. It was taken by the Crusaders in 1100, and retaken by the Saracens in 1187. In 1191 it was recovered by the Crusaders (under Guido of Jerusalem, Philip of France, and Richard the Lion-hearted of England), and held by them till they were finally driven out of Palestine in 1291. It was the last fortified place wrested from the Christians by the Turks.

Aholiab—A skillful artificer of the tribe of Dan, who was appointed, together with Bezaleel, to construct the tabernacle in the wilderness and the ark of the covenant.

Amalekites—A nomadic and warlike people, occupying, at the time of the Exodus, the Sinaitic peninsula and the wilderness between Egypt and Palestine. They lived generally in migrating parties, in caves or tents, like the Bedaween Arabs of the present day. The Israelites had scarcely passed the Red Sea when the Amalekites attacked them at Rephidim, and slew those who, through fatigue or weakness, lagged behind, but were signally defeated in the final attack. They came again into conflict with a part of the Israelites on the border of the promised land; and after four hundred years Saul attacked and destroyed the greater part of them. The remnant that escaped, David defeated on several occasions; and finally they were blotted out by the Simeonites in the time of Hezekiah.

Ammonites—They were the descendants of Ammon, or Ben-Ammi, the son of Lot by his youngest daughter (Gen. xix. 38). They destroyed an ancient race of giants called Zamzummim, and seized their country, which lay east of the Jordan between the rivers Arnon and Jabbok, and adjoining the northern part of Moab. Their chief city was Robbah, which stood on the Jabbok, fifty-five miles E. NE. of Jerusalem. Yet in the time of Moses they had been driven out of this region, toward the east, by the Amorites. About the year 1187 B. C. the Ammonites greatly oppressed the Israelites, and Jephthah, who had been expelled from home by his brothers on account of his illegitimate birth and gone to the land of Tob, a district beyond the Jordan, where he had become the chief of a band of brigands, was invited by the Israelites to become their commander. He accepted the invitation on the condition that he should remain their ruler if he defeated the Ammonites. The victory was complete, and hence he ruled or was judge over the country the rest of his life. A most affecting incident in his life was his devoting his daughter to God as a sacrifice in consequence of a rash vow (Judg. xi.).

Amorites—A people descended from Emer, the fourth son of Canaan (Gen. x. 10). They first peopled the mountains west of the Dead Sea, near Hebron; but afterwards extended their limits and took possession of the finest provinces of Moab and Ammon, on the east between the brooks of Jabbok and Arnon. Moses took this country from their king Sihon. The lands which the Amorites possessed on the west side of the Jordan were given to the tribe of Judah, and those on the east, to the tribes of Reuben and Gad. The Amorites were afterwards subdued by Joshua, but he was not able to exterminate them. They appear to have been long hostile to the Israelites, but in Solomon's time were reduced to a tributary condition.

Antioch—An ancient city and the former capital of Syria, situated on a fertile and beautiful plain on the left bank of the river Orontes. It was founded in 301 B. C., and named after Antiochus, a general in the Syrian army and father of Seleucus Nicator, the founder of the Syrian monarchy. It was the favorite residence of the kings of Syria and was called "Antioch the Beautiful." It was widely celebrated for the splendor of its luxury and the magnificence of its palaces and temples. The population in the time of its greatest prosperity is supposed to have been 400,000 or more. It has been visited by several earthquakes and is now nearly ruined. The disciples of Christ were first called Christians in Antioch, which occupies a prominent position in the history of the primitive church as the scene of the labors of the apostle Paul. The Crusaders took Antioch from the Saracens in 1098, after which it was the capital of a Christian principality until 1269. Its situation, amid innumerable groves and small streams, midway between Alexander and Constantinople, rendered it a place of great beauty and salubrity, as well as commercial importance. Among the remains of its former grandeur are the ruined walls and aqueduct.

Arabia—Is a country of western Asia, lying south and east of Judea. It is divided into three parts—Deserta, Petræa and Felix. *Arabia Deserta* is a vast steppe or elevated expanse of sand, with occasional hills and a sparse vegetation. It has the mountains of Gilead on the west, and the river Euphrates on the east, and extends far to the south. *Arabia Petraea* lies south of the Holy Land and had Petra for its capital. This region contained the Edomites and Amalekites, etc., people at present known under the general name of Arabs. *Arabia Felix* lies still farther south and east, and does not immediately adjoin the Holy Land. The Queen of Sheba, who visited Solomon, was probably queen of part of Arabia Felix. This country abounded with riches, particularly with spices, and is now called Hedjar. It is much celebrated in modern times by reason of the cities of Mecca and Medina being situated in it. There are, according to native historians, two races of Arabs; those who derive their descent from the primitive inhabitants of the land, Joktan, a son of Eber, and by him connected with the Hebrews and other Shemitic families, and those who claim Ishmael as their ancestor. They are Mohammedans, but their religion sets but lightly on them.

Arabia Deserta—See ARABIA.

Arabia Petraea—See ARABIA.

Arabia Felix—See ARABIA.

Aram-Naha-raim—See MESOPOTAMIA.

Ark of the Covenant—In the year 1116 B. C. the ark was taken from Shiloh to Ebenezer; there the Philistines captured the Israelites and took the ark to Ashdod and set it in the house of Dagon; it was then taken to Gath.

and from there to Ekron. In 1115 B. C. it was taken to the land of Beth-shemesh, and from there to Kirjath-jearim, a city of the Gibeonites, about nine miles northeast of Jerusalem, and placed in the house of Abinadab, a Levite (I. Sam. iv.-vii.). In 1045 B. C. the ark was taken to the house of Obed-edom, a Gentile (II. Sam. vi.-x.), and in the same year it was carried under King David's instructions to Jerusalem, where it was placed in a temporary tabernacle (I. Chron. xv., xvi.).

Athelstan—An able Anglo-Saxon king of England, born about 895 A. D., was the natural son of Edward the Elder, and a grandson of Elfred the Great. He began to reign in 925, and was the first actual sovereign of all England. On the death of Sigtric, king of Northumbria, Athelstan annexed that country. A league was formed against him by the Welsh, Scots and Picts, whom he defeated in a great battle at Brunenburg, in 937. He reigned over nearly all the island, except Scotland and Wales. He promoted learning and civilization, and was reputed one of the wisest of the Anglo-Saxon kings. He died without issue October 27, 940, and was succeeded by his brother Edmund.

Athanasius—Saint, a celebrated Greek Father of the church, was born at Alexandria about A. D. 296. His education was directed by Alexander, archbishop of Alexandria. After he had been ordained as a deacon he was appointed a member of the General Council of Nice (A. D. 325), in which he distinguished himself by his eloquence, learning, and zeal against Arianism (a denial that the Son was co-essential and co-eternal with the Father).

Bacchus (Gr., *Dionysus*)—The youthful and beautiful god of wine, said to be the son of Jupiter. He taught men the culture of the vine, and first produced from grapes an intoxicating drink. His worship was spread over many countries of the world, and the myth of Bacchus was variously modified by different peoples.

Baldwyn Encampment—An original Encampment of Knights Templar at Bristol, in England, said to have been established from time immemorial. (No doubt the Masonified [excuse the term] lineal descendant of the Preceptories of the thirteenth century. See Knights Templar, Masonic, page 152.) Four other Encampments of the same character are said to have existed in London, Bath, York and Salisbury. The Knights of Bristol were well-to-do and had large possessions in that ancient city. In the eighteenth century the Duke of Sussex received from the "Order of the Temple," at Paris, the degree of Knights Templar and the authority to establish a Grand Conclave in England. He did so; and convened that body once, only once. His authority came from the Templars of France, who professed to have continued the Order by authority of a charter given by James de Molay to Larmenius. During the remaining years of his life as Grand Master, Templarism had no activity in England, for he, for some cause or other, discountenanced all Christian and chivalric Masonry. After his death some of his officers and followers resolved to rescue the Order from its degraded position, and several of the Encampments met and formed the Grand Conclave of England.

In the meantime, of the five original Encampments of England, who claimed to be the genuine representatives of the Knights of the Temple, four had expired, leaving Bristol the sole relic of the Order, with the exception of the Encampments that had been created in various parts of the country, not holding under any legitimate authority, but raised by Knights who had been created in the Baldwyn Encampment at Bristol.

Under these circumstances the Knights of Baldwyn, feeling that their place was at the head of the Order, would not yield precedence to the Encampment of Observance (the original Encampment of the Duke of Sussex), derived from a foreign and spurious source, the so-called Order of the Temple in Paris, and refused to send representatives to the forming of the Grand Conclave of England. They also refused to acknowledge its authority in Bristol until such time as their claim should be treated with the consideration they believed it deserved.

In 1857 the Knights at Bristol sought a reconciliation with the Grand Conclave of England, but were refused. They then in the same year "revived" the "Ancient Supreme Grand and Royal Encampment of Masonic Knights Templar," with a constituency of seven bodies. But this body did not have a very long existence, for in 1860 the Camp at Baldwyn surrendered its independence, and became a recognized constituent of the Grand Conclave of England and Wales.

Belshazzar—Was the son of Nabonadius, the sixth and last king of the second Babylonian period. His mother was a daughter of Nebuchadnezzar, and probably the widow of Neriglissar, the fourth king of the period. When of sufficient age he was associated with his father on the throne, and in the Book of Daniel is therefore called king. The night of the fall of Babylon, 538 B. C., he made an impious feast, at which he and his courtiers drank out of the sacred vessels which had been carried away from the temple at Jerusalem by Nebuchadnezzar. He was terrified by the apparition of the hand which wrote upon the wall; and in the same night was slain, and the city taken by Cyrus of Persia. The importance of Babylon rapidly declined soon after its capture by Cyrus, for he made Susa the capital of his kingdom. "There was a town on its site until the fourth century, and many Jews dwelt there." But from this time onward Babylon ceases almost to be mentioned; even its ruins have not been discovered until within the last two centuries. It is infested by noxious animals, and perhaps in no place under heaven is the contrast between ancient magnificence and present desolation greater than here.

Bethany—A village on the eastern slope of Mount Olivet, about two miles east-southeast of Jerusalem, and on the road to Jericho. It was often visited by Christ. Here Martha and Mary dwelt. It was from the midst of His disciples, near this village which he loved, that Christ ascended to heaven

Bethlehem—A celebrated city in the tribe of Judah, six miles south of Jerusalem. It was beautifully situated on an oblong ridge, twenty-seven hundred feet above the level of the sea, and affording a fine view in every direction. The hills around it were terraced, and clothed with vines, fig trees, and almonds; and the valleys around it bore rich crops of grain. Its memory is delightfully associated with the names of Boaz and Ruth; it is celebrated as the birthplace and city of David; but, above all, it is hallowed as the place where the Redeemer was born. Over that lonely spot the guiding star hovered; there the eastern sages worshiped the King of kings, and there, where David watched his flock and praised God, were heard the songs of the angelic host at the Saviour's birth.

Birthright—The privilege of the first-born son. Among the Hebrews, as indeed among most other nations, the first-born enjoyed particular privileges; and wherever polygamy was tolerated, it was highly necessary to fix them. Besides the father's chief blessing, the first-born son of a priest succeeded his father in the priestly office. Among the sons of Jacob, Reuben, the first-born, forfeited the right of the first-born and it was given to Levi. The first-born was entitled to a share of his father's estate twice as large as any of the other brethren received, and succeeded to the official dignities and rights of his father.

Briton—A native or citizen of ancient Britain or Britannia; a name given to the aboriginal or ancient inhabitants of that island. When Cæsar invaded the island in 55 B. C., he found in it two different peoples—the interior was occupied by the primitive or indigenous Celtic inhabitants, who had been driven back from the coasts by a people of probable Gothic descent. The latter had colonized the southeast part of the island, and were less numerous than the Celtic Britons. Cæsar was the first who gave the name Britannia to this island, which before his time was called Albion. The language of the southern Celtic Britons was very similar to the present Welsh. "The Gauls and Britons," says R. G. Lotham, "are fundamental populations of the British Isles." The Picts were either aboriginal or intrusive. If aboriginal, they were, like the Gauls and Britons, Celtic. The religion of the island was Druidism.

Byblos—A seaport and district of Phœnicia, north of Beyroot, whose Scriptural or Hebrew name was Gebal. The inhabitants were called Giblites, and denoted in the Hebrew word rendered "stone-squarers" in I. Kings v. 18. Their land and all Lebanon were assigned to the Israelites, but never fully possessed. It was an important place, and the seat of the worship of Thammuz.

Caesarea—A city situated on the coast of the Mediterranean Sea, between Joppa and Tyre. It was anciently a small place called the Tower of Strato, but rebuilt with great splendor, and strongly fortified by Herod the Great, who formed a harbor by constructing a vast breakwater, adorned the city with many stately buildings, and named it Cæsarea in honor of Cæsar. This city was the capital of Judea during the reign of Herod the Great and of Herod Agrippa I., and was also the seat of the Roman power while Judea was governed as a province of the empire. It is now a heap of ruins.

Canaan—The land peopled by Canaan, the son of Ham and grandson of Noah (Gen. ix. 18). His numerous posterity seem to have occupied Zidon first, and thence spread in Syria and Canaan. This country has at different periods been called by various names, either from its inhabitants or some circumstances connected with its history.

(1) "The land of Canaan," from Canaan, who divided it among his sons, each of whom became the head of a numerous tribe, and ultimately of a distinct people. This did not at first include any land east of the Jordan (Gen. x., xi.).

(2) "The land of promise," from the promise given to Abraham that his posterity should possess it (Heb. xi. 9; Gen. xii. 7).

(3) These being termed Hebrews, the region in which they dwelt was called "the land of the Hebrews" (Gen. xl. 15).

(4) "The land of Israel," from the Israelites, or posterity of Jacob, having settled there. This name comprehends all that tract of ground, on each side of the Jordan, which God gave for an inheritance to the Hebrews. At a later age this term was often restricted to the territory of the ten tribes (Ezek. xxvii. 17).

(5) "The land of Judah." This at first comprised only the region which was allotted to the tribe of Judah. After the separation of the ten tribes, the land which belonged to Judah and Benjamin, who formed a separate kingdom, was distinguished by the appellation of "the land of Judah," or Judea, which latter name the whole country retained during the existence of the second temple, and under the dominion of the Romans.

(6) "Holy Land." This name appears to have been used by the Hebrews after the Babylonish captivity (Zech. xv. 14).

(7) "Palestine" (Ex. xv. 14), a name derived from the Philistines, who settled on the borders of the Mediterranean. A name subsequently given to the whole country. though the Philistines in fact possessed only a small part of it. By

heathen writers, the Holy Land has been variously termed Palestine, Syria and Phœnicia. Canaan was bounded on the west by the Mediterranean Sea, north by Mount Lebanon and Syria, east by Arabia Deserta, and south by Edom and the desert of Zin and Paran. Its extreme length was about one hundred and eighty miles, and its average width about sixty-five. The soil of Canaan was highly productive. Olives, figs, vines and pomegranates grew in abundance; the hills were clothed with flocks and herds, and the valleys were covered with corn. The land of promise was currently described as "flowing with milk and honey." There were eleven tribes, the lineal descendants of the patriarch Canaan.

Canaan was conquered from the Canaanites by the Hebrews under Joshua, 1450 B. C., who divided it into twelve confederate states according to the tribes. Saul united it into one kingdom, and David enlarged its territories. In 975 B. C. it was divided into the kingdoms of Israel and Judah, the latter consisting of the tribes of Judah and Benjamin, and the former of the rest of the tribes. Assyria crushed the northern kingdom of Israel about 721 B. C., and Babylon crushed the southern kingdom of Israel about 588 B. C. Since then the country has been under foreign domination, with hardly more than the shadow of independence at any time. Persians, Greeks and Romans succeeded one another in the mastery. In the time of Christ under the Romans, there were four provinces—Galilee, Samaria and Judea on the west side of the Jordan, and Perea on the east side. Since A. D. 637, when Palestine was conquered by the Saracens, it has, with little interruption, been under Mohammedan power.

Ceres—The Roman name of the goddess of grain, fruit and agriculture; identical with the Grecian Demeter. Ceres was the mother of Proserpine.

Chaldeans—See CHALDEA.

Chaldea—A country in Asia, the capital of which, in its widest extent, was Babylon. It was originally of small extent, but the empire being afterwards very much enlarged, the name is generally taken in a more extensive sense, and includes Babylonia. The Chaldeans were originally a warlike people, who at first inhabited the Koordish Mountains north of Assyria and Mesopotamia. As the Assyrian monarchs extended their conquests toward the north and west, the Chaldeans also came under their dominion; and this rough and energetic people appear to have assumed, under the sway of their conquerors, a new character, and to have been transformed from a rude horde into a civilized people. A very vivid and graphic description of the Chaldean warriors is given by the prophet Habakkuk, who probably lived about that time when they first made incursions into Palestine or the adjacent regions (Hab. i. 6-11). Of the date of their location in Babylonia nothing is now known. The Babylonian Empire was founded by Nimrod 2,000 years before Christ, and then embraced the cities of Babel, Erech, Accad and Calneh. The most ancient name of the country is Shinar; afterwards Babel. Babylon and Babylonia became its common appellation, with which, at a later period, Chaldea, or the land of the Chaldeans, was used as synonymous, after this people had got the whole into their possession. In the reign of King Hezekiah, 713 B. C., a king of Babylon is mentioned, the first of whom we read after Nimrod and Amraphel. About one hundred years later we find the Chaldeans in possession of the kingdom of Babylon. The first sovereign in the new line appearing in history was Nabopolassar. His son Nebuchadnezzar invaded Palestine and he was succeeded by his son Evil-Merodach. After him came, in quick succession, Neriglissar, Laborosoarchod, and Nabonadius or Belshazzar, under whom this empire was absorbed in the Medo-Persian. The Babylonians were the descendants of Shem

Cyrus—Surnamed The Great, was the founder of the Persian Empire. He was the son of Cambyses, king of Persia, and Mandane, daughter of Astyages, king of the Medes. The habits and manners of the two peoples were alike, and the general motives of war were, for the most part, wanting between them. No doubt there was certain dependency—political, and perhaps tributary—of the Persian upon the Median kings. For the purpose of education and to learn refinement of manners, young Cyrus was placed in charge of his grandfather, Astyages, at the court of the Medes. According to a tradition, Astyages was alarmed by a dream which portended that the offspring of Mandane would become king, or conquer Media, and he commanded an officer named Harpagus to kill Cyrus. Harpagus promised to obey the order, but privily committed the boy to the care of a herdsman, who brought him up with his own children. Cyrus, having discovered the secret of his birth and having inured himself to the hardy habits of the warlike Persians, incited the latter to revolt against the King of Media. With the encouragement and assistance of his father, who was killed during the great battle, he defeated Astyages, destroyed his army and took him prisoner. The victory was so complete and overwhelming that his chiefs and generals gathered around him on the battlefield and proclaimed him *King of Media and Persia.* During his reign, among the many of his exploits was the capture of Babylon in 538 B. C. In 536 B. C. he issued that famous edict whereby the Jewish captives who had been deported to Babylon were permitted to return to Jerusalem and rebuild their temple.

Herodotus states that Cyrus afterwards invaded the country of the Scythians, who were ruled by Queen Tomyris, and that he gained several victories over her, but was drawn into an ambush and killed in 529 B. C. He was succeeded by his son Cambyses.

The kingdoms of Persia, Media and Babylon were connected by royal family ties from the time of Nabopolassar to that of Darius, by the marriage of Nebuchadnezzar, son of Nabopolassar and King of Babylon, to Amyitis, daughter of Astyages, King of Media. Cambyses, King of Persia, married Mandane, daughter of Astyages, King of Media. Cyrus the Great was the son of King Cambyses and Mandane and the grandson of Astyages, King of Media. Belshazzar was the son of Nabonadius, King of Babylon, and the grandson of Nebuchadnezzar.

Damascus—A celebrated metropolis of Syria, and now probably the oldest city on the globe. It stands on the river Barada, in a beautiful and fertile plain on the east and southeast of Ante-Lebanon. This plain is about fifty miles in circumference; it is open to the desert of Arabia on the south and east, and is bounded on the other sides by the mountains. It is still celebrated, with the surrounding country, by all travelers as one of the most beautiful and luxuriant regions in the world. The Orientals themselves call it the "Paradise on earth." It is the most purely Oriental city yet remaining of all that are named in the Bible. Its public buildings and bazaars are fine; and many private dwellings, though outwardly mean, are decorated within in a style of the most costly luxury. Its position has made it from the very first a commercial city; huge caravans assemble here at intervals, and traverse, just as of old, the desert routes to remote cities.

Darius, King of Persia—The successor of Cyrus and Cambyses (Ahasuerus) on the throne of Persia, Babylon and Media, was the son of Hystaspes, a member of the noble family of Achæmenidæ. He was one of the seven noble Persians who conspired against and killed the usurper Smerdis (Artaxerxes), whom he succeeded in 521 B. C. He married two daughters of Cyrus the Great, and organized the extensive empire which Cyrus and Cambyses had enlarged by conquest. He preserved the friendly policy of his predecessor Cyrus, in reference to the Jews, and confirmed the decrees of that monarch, which had been revoked during the reign of Artaxerxes, by a new edict. In the second year of his reign, Haggai and Zechariah, encouraged by this edict, induced their countrymen to resume the work of restoring the temple, which was finished four years afterwards. Darius died in the year 485 B. C. and was succeeded by his son Xerxes.

Darius the Median—See Book of Daniel, chaps. v., vi.

Desert, or Wilderness—The Scriptures, by desert, generally mean an uncultivated place, a wilderness, or grazing tract. Some deserts were actually dry and barren; others were beautiful, and had good pastures. David speaks of the beauty of the desert (Psa. lxv. 12, 13).

Desert of Kadish—See Wilderness of Paran.

Desert of Zin—See Wilderness of Paran.

Dionysus—See Bacchus.

Edom (Gr., *Idumea*)—See Edomites.

Edomites—They were the descendants of Jacob's twin brother Esau (called Edom), and inhabited a territory bounded on the north by Judea and on the west by the Mediterranean Sea. It was called Edom, or, in Greek, Idumea. At one time it comprised parts of Judea as far north as Hebron, and in Arabia the peninsula of Petræa. It was annexed to Judea by David and later by the Maccabees. The relations between the Jews and the Edomites were always hostile and full of hatred, even after the Jews had received an Edomite dynasty in the son of Herod the Great, in whose time the Edomites were, however, Jews in religion (Gen. xxxvi.).

Fatimites—A family of Arabian caliphs, who took their name from the fact that they claimed descent from Fatima.

the daughter of the prophet Mohammed. They ruled from 909 till 1171, chiefly at Cairo, and at the period of their widest sway ruled all north Africa, with Syria and Palestine.

Feasts—The Jews have established several festivals, or days of rest and worship, to perpetuate the memory of great events wrought in their early history: the *Sabbath* commemorated the creation of the world; the *Passover,* the departure out of Egypt, because, the night before their departure, the destroying angel, who slew the first-born of the Egyptians, passed over the houses of the Hebrews without entering them, they being marked by the blood of the lamb; the *Pentecost,* celebrated the fiftieth day after the sixteenth day of Nisan, which was the second day of the feast of the Passover. The Hebrews call it the "feast of weeks," because it was kept seven weeks after the Passover. It was instituted, first, to oblige the Israelites to repair to the temple of the Lord, and there acknowledge his dominion over their country and their labors, by offering to Him the firstfruits of all their harvests. Secondly, to commemorate, and to render thanks to God for the law given from Mount Sinai, on the fiftieth day after their coming out of Egypt. The *Tabernacle* was instituted in memory of the forty years' wanderings of the Israelites in the desert, and also as a season of gratitude and thanksgiving for the gathering in of the harvest; whence it is also called the Feast of the Harvest. At the three great feasts of the year, the Passover, Pentecost, and that of Tabernacles, all the males of the nation were required to visit the temple. The other festivals were the Feast of *Trumpets* (or *New Moon*), *Purim, Dedication,* the *Sabbath Year* and the *Year of Jubilee.* The Hebrews were a hospitable people, and were wont to welcome their guests with a feast and dismiss them with another. The returning prodigal was thus welcomed. Many joyful domestic events were observed with feasting—birthdays, marriages, sheep-shearing and harvesting. During the repast and after it various entertainments were provided; enigmas were proposed, eastern tales were told; music and hired dancers, and often excessive drinking, etc., occupied the time.

Feast of the Passover—See FEASTS.

Feast of the Pentecost—See FEASTS.

Feast of the Sabbath—See FEASTS.

Feast of the Tabernacle—See FEASTS.

Gedaliah—A son of Ahikam, appointed by Nebuchadnezzar to govern Judea after the destruction of Jerusalem. Like his father, he honored and befriended Jeremiah. He began the administration of his government at Mizpeh with wisdom, but in two months was treacherously murdered by one Ishmael (Jer. xli.).

Gibeonites—See GIBEON.

Gibeon—A city of the Hivites (descendants of Canaan), afterwards a Levitical city in the tribe of Benjamin. It lay near Geba and Gebeah, and is sometimes wrongly taken for Geba. Its Canaanite inhabitants secured a treaty with Joshua and the elders of Israel by stratagem, and were made hewers of wood for the sanctuary. Here the tabernacle was set up for many years. It stood on an eminence, six miles north of Jerusalem. The inhabitants were called Gibeonites.

Goshen—See LAND OF GOSHEN.

Haran—An ancient city, called in the New Testament Charran, situated in the northwest part of Mesopotamia. Here, after leaving Ur, Abraham dwelt till his father Terah died; and to this old homestead Isaac sent for a wife, and Jacob fled from the wrath of Esau. Haran was ravaged by the Assyrians in the time of Hezekiah (713 B. C.). Here also Crassus, the Roman general, was defeated and killed by the Parthians (53 B. C.). The Parthians were great horsemen and would seem to have borne no very distant resemblance to the modern Cossacks. It is said they were either refugees or exiles from the Scythian nation. Harran, as it is now called, is situated on a branch of the Euphrates, in a flat and sandy plain, and is only peopled by a few wandering Arabs, who select it for the delicious water it furnishes.

Hebrews—That branch of the posterity of Abraham whose home was in the land of promise. The name Hebrew is first applied to Abraham in Gen. xv. 13, and is generally supposed to have been derived from Heber, the last of the long-lived patriarchs. Heber outlived six generations of his descendants, including Abraham himself, after whose death he was for some years the only surviving ancestor of Isaac and Jacob. Hebrews appears to have been the name by which the Jewish people was known to foreigners, in distinction from their common domestic name, "the children of Israel." The name of Jews, derived from Judah, was afterwards applied to them as inhabitants of Judea.

Hebron—On of the most ancient cities of Canaan, being built seven years before Tanis, the capital of Lower Egypt. It was anciently called Mamre, and was a favorite residence of the patriarchs Abraham, Isaac and Jacob. Here, too, they were buried. Under Joshua and Caleb the Israelites conquered it from the Canaanites, and it was afterwards made a Levitical city of refuge. It was David's seat of government during the seven years when he reigned over Judah only. Here Absalom raised the standard of revolt. It was fortified by Rehoboam, the son and successor of Solomon.

At present Hebron is an unwalled city of about 8,000 inhabitants, of whom some 600 are Jews and the remainder Turks and Arabs. It lies in a deep valley and on the adjacent hillside, in the ancient hill country of Judea, about twenty miles south of Jerusalem. Its modern name, El-

Khulil, is the same which the Moslems give to Abraham,
"the friend of God"; and they profess to hold in their
keeping the burial-place of the patriarchs, the "cave of
Machpelah." It is covered by a small mosque surrounded
by a stone structure 60 feet high, 150 feet wide, and 200
feet long. Within this no Christian is permitted to enter;
but it is evidently of very high antiquity, and may well
be regarded as enclosing the true site of the ancient tomb.
The environs of the city are very fertile, furnishing the
finest vineyards in Palestine, numerous plantations of olive
and other fruit trees and excellent pasturage.

Horus—The child of Osiris and Isis. He came into the
world to avenge his father. As a youth he takes the name
of Buto. Then he becomes the Strong Horus, the great
helper, the pillar of the world. Horus was the god of light,
turning the gloom of winter into the verdure and life of
spring.

Holy Land—See CANAAN (Par. 6).

Ishmael—See ISHMAELITES.

Ishmaelites—The descendants of Ishmael, the son of
Abraham and Hagar, who was born in the year 1910 B. C.
Hagar was the Egyptian handmaid of Abraham's wife
Sarah. Ishmael was at first regarded as "the son of the
promise," but after the birth and weaning of Isaac, he was
driven from his father's house, at the age of about seventeen,
and with his mother took their way towards Egypt, her native land. Overcome with heat and thirst, and then miraculously relieved (Gen. xxi.), he remained in the wilderness of
Paran, "and his mother took him a wife out of the land of
Egypt," and he became the father of twelve sons, heads of
Arab tribes. He seems to have become on friendly terms
with Isaac, and to have attended at the bedside of their dying
father. At his own death he was 137 years old. The
Ishmaelites were said in the days of Moses to have dwelt in

the northwestern part of Arabia. Subsequently they, with the descendants of Joktan, the fourth son of Shem, and Joksham, the son of Abraham by Keturah, occupied the whole peninsula of Arabia. Located near their "brethren" the Jews, they have always led a roving, wild and predatory life. To a great degree unchanged, they are to this day the untamed though tributary masters of the desert.

Jebusites—See JERUSALEM.

Jericho—Once one of the most flourishing cities of Palestine, seven miles westward from the Jordan and eighteen miles northeast from Jerusalem. Westward from Jericho lies a waste tract of limestone mountains rising in stages; but the immediate vicinity is well watered and fruitful, yielding dates, raisins, etc.; in early times a favorite abode of poisonous snakes. The capture of Jericho by the Israelites on their first entry into Canaan, its destruction and the rebuilding of it by Hiel the Bethelite in the reign of Ahab, about 918 B. C., are found recorded in Joshua vi.: I. Kings xvi. 34. It appears to have been afterwards the seat of a school of prophets, and was the residence of Elisha. Herod the Great resided in Jericho and beautified it. In the time of the Crusades it was repeatedly captured and at last completely destroyed. At the present day its place is occupied by a miserable village called Richa or Erisha The road from Jericho to Jerusalem ascends through narrow and rocky passes amid ravines and precipices. It is an exceedingly difficult and dangerous route, and is still infested by robbers, as in the time of the good Samaritan (Luke x. 30-34).

Jerusalem—Its origin and early history are very obscure. The Jebusites, who were the descendants of Canaan, were the first known occupants of that elevated ground upon which rests the city, which they called Jebus, and we know that the Jebusites retained possession of the strong position of the hill of Zion for a considerable time after the conquest of Canaan, and even after the storming of Jerusalem, while the tribes of Judah and Benjamin occupied the lower city. They were finally dispossessed by David. The name of Jerusalem is first mentioned in Josh. x. 1. It lies upon the original border of Judah and Benjamin, the line of which runs through the Valley of Hinnom, so that Zion and the northern city lay within the territory of Benjamin. Its historical importance dates from the time of David, who there fixed his residence, calling it by the name of the "City of David," transporting to it the ark of the covenant. The building of the temple under Solomon was the consummation of the dignity and holiness of Jerusalem, which was further enlarged, strengthened, and beautified by this king and his successors. It suffered a diminution of political importance through the revolt and secession of the ten tribes, from which date its history is identified with that of the kingdom of Judah. It was pillaged (971 B. C.) by Shishak, King of Egypt; by Joash, King of Israel; and finally (588 B. C.) it was taken, after a siege of three years, by Nebuchadnezzar, who razed its walls and destroyed the temple and palaces by fire. Having been rebuilt after the Captivity (536 B. C.), it was again taken and pillaged under Ptolemy Lagos (320 B. C.), an Egyptian king, who carried thousands away slaves to Egypt. Antiochus IV. succeeded to the throne of Syria in 176 B. C. and deliberately began to plan the extinguishment of the Jewish people. He sent an army to Jerusalem, which entered on a Sabbath day (168 B. C.), made havoc of the inhabitants and leveled the city walls. Pompey took the city (63 B. C.), put 12,000 of the inhabitants to the sword, and razed the walls to the ground. A few years later (56 B. C.) it was pillaged by Crassus; and from these beginnings date the continued series of Roman aggressions, which terminated in the complete destruction of the city and dispersion of the Jewish race under Vespasian and Titus, A. D. 70.

Jethro—"Moses' father-in-law," a shepherd prince or priest of Midian. When the Hebrews were at Mount Sinai he visited Moses, gave him some wise counsel as to the government of the tribes, and then returned to his own people. Jethro was a worshiper of God, and some infer that he was a descendant of Abraham through Midian.

Jones, Inigo—One of the most celebrated of English architects and hence called the Vitruvius of England. He was born at London July 15, 1573, and died June 21, 1652, in the seventy-ninth year of his age. He was successively the architect of three kings—James I., Charles I. and Charles II., and during his long career superintended the erection of many of the most magnificent public and private edifices in England, among which was the old church of St. Paul's. He was elected Grand Master under James I. in 1607. During his administration several learned men were initiated into the Order, and the society considerably increased in consequence and reputation. The Communications of the Fraternity were established, and the annual festivals regularly observed.

Joppa—One of the most ancient seaports in the world. It was a border town of the tribe of Dan, on the coast of the Mediterranean Sea, about thirty-five miles northwest of Jerusalem. Here, according to the classical myth, it was that Andromeda was chained to the rock, and expoesd to the sea monster; a story that has been supposed to shadow out in an obscure way, the early intercourse between Greece and Syria. Its harbor is shoal and unprotected from the winds; but on account of its convenience to Jerusalem it became the principal port of Judea and is still the great landing place of pilgrims. Here the materials for building both the first and the second temple, sent from Lebanon and Tyre, were landed. Joppa was twice destroyed by the Romans. It attained its highest prosperity in the times of the Crusades, when it became the principal landing-place of the warriors of Christendom. In 1799 it was stormed and sacked by the French, and twelve hundred Turkish prisoners, said to have broken their parole, were put to death. The present town of Joppa, sometimes called Jaffa, or Yafa, is situated on a promontory jutting out into the sea, rising to the height of about one hundred and fifty feet, crowned with a fortress, and offering on all sides picturesque and varied prospects. The town is walled round on the south and east, toward the land, and partially so on the north and west, toward the sea. The inhabitants are mostly Turks and Arabs.

Joseph of Arimathea—A native of Arimathea, but at the time of Christ's crucifixion a resident of Jerusalem. He was a member of the Jewish Sanhedrim, and opposed in vain their action in condemning the Saviour (Luke xxiii. 51). When all was over he "went in boldly unto Pilate, and craved the body of Jesus." It was now night and the Jewish Sabbath was at hand. He therefore, with the aid of Nicodemus, wrapped the body in spices for the time, and laid it in his own tomb.

Kabbalah—The mystical philosophy or theosophy of the Jews is called the Kabbalah. The word is derived from the Hebrew *kabal*, signifying to receive, because it is the doctrine received from the elders. Practically speaking, the doctrine of Kabbalah refers to the system handed down by oral transmission, and is nearly allied to *tradition*. It has sometimes been used in an enlarged sense, as comprehending all the explanations, maxims and ceremonies which have been traditionally handed down to the Jews; but in that more limited acceptation in which it is intimately connected with the symbolic science of Freemasonry, the Kabbalah may be defined to be a system of philosophy which embraces certain mystical interpretations of Scripture, and metaphysical speculations concerning the Deity, man, and spiritual beings. In these interpretations and speculations, according to the Jewish doctors, were enveloped the most profound truths of religion, which, to be comprehended by finite beings, are obliged to be revealed through the medium of symbols and allegories. ✦

Kadesh-Barnea—See WILDERNESS OF PARAN.

Kingdom of Judah—See CANAAN (Par. 5).

Land of Canaan—See CANAAN (Par. 1).

Land of Chaldeans—See CHALDEA.

Land of Goshen—The land of Goshen appears to have been that tract of country in Egypt which was inhabited by the Israelites from the time of Jacob to that of Moses. It was probably the tract lying east of the Pelusian arm of the Nile, toward Arabia. Ramses was the capital of Goshen, a city built by the Hebrews during their servitude in Egypt. From it they commenced their united exodus from Egypt. It is thought to have been on the line of the ancient canal from the Nile to the Red Sea, and some thirty-five miles northwest of Suez. In this district, or adjacent to it, was the city of On, or Heliopolis. The inhabitants of Egypt may be considered as including three divisions: the Copts, or descendants of the ancient Egyptians; the Fellahs, or husbandmen, who are supposed to represent the people in Scripture called Phul; the Arabs, or conquerors of the country, including the Turks, etc. Its early history is involved in great obscurity. Their religion consisted in the worship of heavenly bodies and the powers of nature. The priests were the most honored and powerful of the castes into which the people were divided.

Land of Hebrews—See CANAAN (Par. 3).

Land of Israel—See CANAAN (Par. 4).

Land of Judah—See CANAAN (Par. 5).

Land of Promise—See CANAAN (Par. 2).

Land of Shinar—See CHALDEA.

Lot—The son of Haran, and nephew of Abraham, followed his uncle from Ur, and afterwards from Haran, to settle in Canaan. Abraham always had a great affection for him, and when they could not continue longer together in Canaan, because they both had large flocks and their shepherds sometimes quarreled, he gave Lot the choice of his abode. Lot chose the plain of Sodom, which appears then to have been the most fertile part of the land. Here he continued to dwell until the destruction of Sodom and the adjacent cities (Gen. xix.).

Mesopotamia—The Greek name of the country between the rivers Euphrates and the Tigris, northwest of Babylonia. In Hebrew, "Aram-Naha-raim" (Aram of the two rivers), or "Padan-aram" (the plain of Aram), or simply Padan (the plain), in distinction from the "Mountains" of Aram. *Aram*, in Hebrew, is synonymous with Syria, a large district of Asia, lying, in the widest acceptation of the name, northeast of Palestine, extending from the river Tigris on the east, nearly to the Mediterranean on the west, and to the Taurus range on the north. It was named after Aram, the son of Shem. Thus defined, it includes also Mesopotamia; that is, in Hebrew, Syria of the two rivers. Mesopotamia is a region associated with the earliest history of the human race both before and after the flood. Eden was not far off; Ararat was near to it on the north, and the land of Shinar on the south. The traveler here reaches what is truly "the old world," and is surrounded by objects compared with which the antiquities of Greece and Rome are modern novelties. This was the home of the patriarchs who preceded Abraham—Terah, Heber, Peleg, etc. Here Abraham and Sarah were born, and the wives of Isaac and Jacob, and most of the sons of Jacob, the heads of twelve tribes. Mesopotamia is also mentioned in Scripture as the abode of the first oppressor of Israel in the times of the judges (Judg. iii, 8-10); and in the history of the wars of David (II. Sam. x. 16).

Middle Ages—These are supposed by the best historians to extend from the year 400 B. C. to the end of the fifteenth century, the last important event being the doubling of the Cape of Good Hope in 1497.

Midianites—An ancient Arabian race, numerous and rich in flocks, herds and camels, the descendants of Midian, the fourth of the six sons of Abraham by Keturah (Isa. lx. 6). They appear to have dwelt mainly to the south of Moab, and covered a territory extending to the neighborhood of Mount Sinai. Midianites were idolators, and often led Israel astray to worship their gods. They also not unfrequently rendered the Hebrews tributary and oppressed them. Often when the Israelites had sown, and their harvest was nearly ready to be gathered in, the Midianites and Amalekites came down like locusts in countless swarms, with their cattle and tents and camels to devour and carry off the fruits of the ground, and not only rob but destroy their owners. And often did the Jews, lacking the strength or the faith or the leadership necessary for effectual resistance, seek refuge in mountain dens and caverns till the invaders retired. Gideon was their deliverer in one such period of oppression (Judg. vi. 7). The Tawarah Arabs, now dwelling in the Sinaitic peninsula, are supposed to be their descendants.

Moabites—They were the descendants of Moab, the son of Lot by his eldest daughter (Gen. xix. 37). An idolatrous people, they were hostile to the Israelites, in spite of the relationship between them. The southern boundary of the Moabites was the brook Zered, which empties into the southeast corner of the Dead Sea. Their territory was about twenty miles from east to west, and at one time extended as far north (fifty miles) as the mountains of Gilead. They were subdued by David, but regained their independence after the dismemberment of the Hebrew kingdom, and disappeared from history after the conquest of

Nebuchadnezzar (604-561 B. C.). The Moabite Stone, which celebrates the achievements of one of their kings, Masha (about 900 B. C.), is one of the most interesting discoveries of modern times. It was found Aug. 19, 1868, by the Rev. Mr. Klein, at Dhiban, just north of the Arnon, and is now in London. (See ROSETTA STONE.)

Monk—Originally, a man who retired from the world for religious meditation and the practice of religious duties in solitude; a religious hermit; in later years, a member of a community or fraternity of men formed for the practice of religious devotions and duties, and bound by the vows of poverty, celibacy and obedience to a superior; specifically, a regular male denizen of a monastery. The term monastery strictly includes the abbey, the priory, nunnery and the friary, and in this broad sense is synonymous with convent. Communities of a more or less monastic character in Palestine and Egypt before the diffusion of Christianity were the Essence and Therapeutæ.

Essences were mystics, and most of them were celibates. The greater part of them lived by themselves near the northwest shore of the Dead Sea. The first distinct trace of them is about 110 B. C., and they disappear from history after the destruction of Jerusalem by the Romans.

Therapeutæs were kindred to, though distinct from, the Essences. Their chief seat was on Lake Marcotis in Egypt. They were not strictly celibate, but rejected wine and animal food.

The ordinary Christian life of the first three centuries, even when not celibate, was largely ascetic and in communities. Christian monasticism in a definite form originated in Upper Egypt in the third or fourth century with St. Anthony, an eminent anchorite, who is called its founder. The first monks were anchorites; those who lived alone, in caves and solitary places in the deserts of Palestine, Egypt and Syria, to which, in some cases, they were driven by persecution. The first monastery was founded by Pachomius on the island of Tabenna in the Nile, about the year 340; the first nunnery by his sister some eight years later. Various developments of the monastic system are to be found in the Middle Ages, as the military orders, friars (often distinguished from monks proper), etc. Since the Reformation, and especially since the French Revolution, monachism has declined in Western countries, or has been overshadowed by the society of Jesuits (a religious order of the Roman Catholic Church), but still continues to flourish in Eastern churches.

Moses—The son of Amram and Jochebed, of the tribe of Levi, and the younger brother of Miriam and Aaron, was born about 1571 B. C. His history is divided into three periods, each of forty years. The first extends from his infancy, when he was exposed in the Nile, and found and adopted by the daughter of Pharaoh, to his flight to Midian. During this time he lived at the Egyptian court, and "was learned in all the wisdom of the Egyptians, and was mighty in words and in deeds" (Acts vii. 22). This is no unmeaning praise: the "wisdom" of the Egyptians, and especially of their priests, was then the profoundest in the world. The second period was from his flight till his return to Egypt, during the whole of which interval he appears to have lived in Midian—it may be much after the manner of the Bedaween sheikhs of the present day. Here he married Zipporah, daughter of the wise and pious Jethro, and became familiar with life in the desert. What a contrast between the former period, spent amid the splendors and learning of a court and this lonely nomadic life. Still it was in this way that he prepared himself to be the instrument of deliverance to his people during the third period of his life, which extends from the exodus out of Egypt to his death on Mount Nebo. The life and institutions of Moses breathe a spirit of freedom, purity, intelligence, justice and humanity elsewhere unknown; and, above all, of supreme love, honor and obedience to God. They molded the character of the Hebrews and transformed them from a nation of shepherds into a people of fixed residence and agricultural habits. Through that people, and through the Bible, the influence of these institutions has been extended over the world; and often where the letter has not been observed the spirit of them has been adopted. Thus it was in the laws established by the Pilgrim Fathers of New England; and no small part of what is of most value in the institutions which they founded is to be ascribed to the influence of the Hebrew legislator. Moses was the author of the Pentateuch, as it is called, or the first five books of the Bible. In the composition of them he was probably assisted by Aaron, who kept a register of public transactions.

Mount Sinai—See SINAI.

Nicodemus—A member of the Jewish Sanhedrim, at first a Pharisee (a Jew, but differing in some points of doctrine and practice), and afterwards a disciple of Jesus. In John vii. 45-52, we see him cautiously defending the Saviour before the Sanhedrim. At last, in the trying scene of the crucifixion, he avowed himself a believer, and came with Joseph of Arimathea to pay the last duties to the body of Christ, which they took down from the cross and laid in the sepulchre.

Olympiad—A period of four years reckoned from one celebration of the Olympic games to another, by which the Greeks computed time from 776 B. C., the reputed first year of the first Olympiad. To turn an Olympiad into a year B. C., multiply by 4. add the year of the Olympiad less 1, and subtract from 780.

Padan-Aram—See MESOPOTAMIA.

Pagan (Paganism)—One who worships false gods. A name for heathenism, originated among the Christians when Christianity gained superiority in the cities and the worship of the old Greek and Roman gods was confined to remote villages (pagi) and the scattered settlers in the country (pagani). It is now used as a general term, including all polytheistic religions (plurality of gods), in opposition to Christianity, Judaism and Mohammedanism; in the Middle Ages it also included Mohammedanism.

Palestine—See CANAAN (No. 7).

Patron—At an early period we find that the Christian church adopted the usage of selecting for every trade and occupation its own patron saint, who is supposed to have taken it under his especial charge. And the selection was generally made in reference to some circumstance in the life of the saint, which traditionally connected him with the profession of which he was appointed the patron. Thus St. Crespin, because he was a shoemaker, is the patron saint of the "gentle craft," and St. Dunstan, who was a blacksmith, is the patron of blacksmiths. Among the ancients every temple, altar, statue or sacred place was dedicated to some divinity. The dedication of a temple was always a festival for the people, and was annually commemorated. While the pagans dedicated their temples to different deities—sometimes to the joint worship of several—the monotheistic (one God) Jews dedicated their religious edifices to the one supreme Jehovah. There was a distinction among the Jews between consecration and dedication, for sacred things were both consecrated and dedicated. This distinction has also been preserved among Christians, many of whom, and, in the early ages, all, consecrated their churches to the worship of God, but dedicated them to, or placed them under, the especial patronage of some particular saint. A similar practice prevails in the Masonic institution; and therefore, while we consecrate our Lodges "to the honor of God's glory," we dedicate them to the patrons of our Order. Tradition informs us that Masonic Lodges were originally dedicated to King Solomon, because he was our first *Most Excellent Grand*

Master. In the sixteenth century St. John the Baptist seems to have been considered as the peculiar patron of Freemasonry; but subsequently this honor was divided between the two Saints John, the Baptist and the Evangelist; and the Modern Lodges, in this country at least, are universally *erected* or *consecrated* to God, and dedicated to the holy Saints John.

Pharaoh—The term applied in the Bible to the kings of Egypt, of which many explanations have been proposed. It seems quite impossible to connect it with the name of any Egyptian monarch, and it must have been a common appellation like Khan, Cæsar or Czar.

Phidias—The greatest sculptor of Greece, perhaps of all ages and lands. He was born at Athens, 500 B. C. He is supposed to have had a long life and to have died from poison about 432 B. C.

Philistines—A people who occupied the southern seacoast of Palestine during most of the period of Biblical history, and were almost constantly at war with the Israelites. As they are not mentioned among the occupants of the land in the time of Joshua, it is inferred that they were later invaders who came from the island of Crete during the obscure early period of the Judges. Their race affinities have been much disputed. The genealogical table in Genesis x. seems to derive them from Ham, through Mizraim, but many commentators nevertheless consider them a Semitic people closely related to the Phœnicians, and not distantly connected with the Israelites themselves. The Philistines shared the fate of the Israelites in successive subjection to Assyria, Babylon and Egypt, and disappeared altogether from history previous to the Christian era.

Phoenicia—See PHOENICIANS.

Phoenicians—A people who occupied a tract of country in the north of Palestine, along the shores of the Mediterranean, of which Tyre and Sidon were the principal cities. The inhabitants themselves called their country Canaan. The history of its people is aphoristic, and in many points utterly insufficient. The Phœnicians have left no literature and no artistic monuments; a few coins and a few inscriptions. They were principally a commercial and not an industrial people. They transferred goods without manufacturing them; they spread the arts without inventing them. Nevertheless, Tyre must have been the seat of considerable industrial skill and activity, since King Hiram could supply Solomon with all kinds of workmen. Modern researches confirm the assertions made that the language spoken by the Jews and the Phœnicians was almost identical; a statement interesting to the Masonic student as giving another reason for the bond which existed between Solomon and Hiram, and between the Jewish workmen and their fellow-laborers of Tyre in the construction of the temple.

Praxiteles—A Greek sculptor, head of the Attic school, born at Athens about 392 B. C. Praxiteles has been called the sculptor of the beautiful, as Phidias was of the sublime.

Proserpine (Gr., *Persephone*)—The daughter of Jupiter and Ceres, wife of Pluto and queen of the infernal regions. She was worshiped generally in connection with her mother, as the goddess of vegetation. She was carried off by Pluto, the god of Hades, to the lower world, but afterward permitted by him to spend half of the year in the upper world.

Queen of Sheba—The land of Sheba of Scripture appears to be the Saba of Strabo, situated towards the southern part of Arabia, at a short distance from the coast of the Red Sea, the capital of which was Mareb. This region, called also Yemen, was probably settled by Sheba, the son of Joktan, of the race of Shem. The Queen of Sheba, who visited Solomon and made him presents of gold, ivory and costly spices, was probably mistress of this region. The tradition of this visit of the Queen of Sheba to Solomon has maintained itself among the Arabs, who call her Balkis, and affirm that she became the wife of Solomon.

Rabbah (Rehoboth)—A city on the Euphrates, south of Carshemish.

Ramses—See LAND OF GOSHEN.

Religion of Masonry—Webster has given two distinct definitions of religion:

1. Recognition of God as an object of worship, love and obedience.

2. Any system of faith and worship.

It is plain that in the first sense in which we may take the word religion, Masonry may rightfully claim to be called a religious institution. No disbeliever in the existence of a God can be made a Mason. All practical piety and performance of the duties we owe to God and to our fellow-men arise from and are founded on a principle of obedience to the divine will. It is idle to say that the Mason does good simply in obedience to the statutes of the Order. These very statutes owe their sanction to the Masonic idea of the nature and perfections of God, which idea has come down to us from earliest history of the institution, and the promulgation of which idea was the very object and design of its origin.

The second definition does not appear to be strictly applicable to Masonry. Masonry has no pretension to assume a place among the religions of the world as a sectarian "system of faith and worship" in the sense in which we distinguish Christianity from Judaism, or Judaism from Mohammedanism. In this meaning of the word we do not and can not speak of the Masonic religion, nor say of a man that he is not a Christian, but a Mason. The tendency of all true Masonry is towards religion. Its ancient landmarks, its sublime ceremonies, its profound symbols and allegories—all inculcate religious doctrine, command religious observance and teach religious truth.

Rephidim—An encampment of the Israelites between the wilderness of Zin, on the east shore of the Gulf of Suez, and Mount Sinai. Here the Amalekites attacked them, and were defeated. It is thought to have been in the valley now called Esh-Sheikh, a day's march northwest of Sinai, and near the western border of the Horeb group of mountains.

Riblah—A city of Syria, in the country of Hamath, at the northeast extremity of Canaan. Its site is probably found in the modern village of Rebleh, on the river Orontes, at the northern end of the great Valley of Lebanon. Through this valley, by way of Hamath and Riblah, was the readiest access to Palestine from the north. At Riblah, in 609 B. C., King Jehoahaz was taken and deposed by Pharaoh-Necho, and carried away captive to Egypt; here also Nebuchadnezzar established his headquarters when warring against Judah. In 588 B. C. he takes and destroys Jerusalem, burns the temple and carries the people, with Zedekiah, whose sons he had slain, captive in chains to Babylon. This terminated the kingdom of Judah, 468 years from the accession of David, 388 years from the revolt of the ten tribes, and 134 years from the ruin of the kingdom of Israel.

Rosetta Stone—In 1799, what is known as the Rosetta Stone was discovered by some of Napoleon's men while making an excavation at Rosetta, in lower Egypt. The stone contained an inscription written in three different characters: first, *Hieroglyphic;* second, *Demotic,* or common character of the Egyptians; third, *Greek.* From the Greek it was discovered that the inscription was tri-lingual; that is, each of the writings was a translation of the others. In 1822 Champollion deciphered the word *Cleopatra* from an obelisk found at Philas. Afterwards, continuing his researches, he completed the translation of the Rosetta Stone, thereby opening up the whole field of Egyptian writings to the long-baffled scholars of the West.

Samaritans—They were originally the descendants of the ten revolting tribes of Israel who had chosen the city of Samaria for their metropolis. Subsequently, the Samaritans were conquered by the Assyrians under Shalmaneser, who carried the greater part of the inhabitants into captivity, and introduced colonists in their place from Babylon, Cultah, Ava and Sepharavain. These colonists, who assumed the name of Samaritans, brought with them, of course, the idolatrous creed and practices of the region from which they emigrated. The Samaritans, therefore, at the time of the rebuilding of the second temple, were an idolatrous race, and as such abhorrent to the Jews (II. Kings xvii. 24-41).

Sanhedrim—Was a council of seventy senators among the Jews, usually with the addition of the high priest as president, who determined the most important affairs of the nation. It was supposed to have originated after the second temple was built, about the year 69 B. C., during the cessation of the prophetic office, and in imitation of Moses' council of seventy elders (Num. xi. 16-24). Jews in foreign cities appear to have been amenable to this court in matters of religion. The right of judging in capital cases belonged to it, until this was taken away by the Romans a few years before the time of Christ. There appears also to have been an inferior tribunal of seven members in every town, for the adjudication of less important matters.

Seljooks, or Seljuks Turks—A small Turkish tribe settled in the plains on the northeastern border of the Caspian Sea, who received their name from Seljook, one of their chiefs, who in the latter part of the tenth century moved in a southeastern direction, conquered Bakjara, and embraced Mohammedanism, and under whose successors they rapidly grew by absorbing other Turkish-Tartarian tribes, and developed a marvelous energy during the course of several centuries. The only source, however, of this energy seems to have been religious fanaticism. About the year 1041 the great Togrol Beg, grandson of Seljook, commenced the invasion of Khorassan and other provinces of Persia, and in 1061 completed the conquest of the whole of Persia, and assumed the title of Sultan. In 1073 Melek Shah, a descendant of Seljook, came into power and conquered Arabia, Syria and Palestine, Asia Minor and Armenia, and ruled from the Mediterranean to the Chinese frontier, and from the Caspian to the Arabian Sea. At his death the Seljook Empire was divided between his four sons, and soon a large number of small, independent sultanates was formed, which circumstance finally caused the ruin of the Seljook dominion. With the overthrow of the Seljook dynasty in 1299, and on the ruins of its dominion, arose the Turkish Empire.

Shechem—A city of central Canaan, thirty-four miles north of Jerusalem. It is first mentioned in the history of Abraham, who here erected his first altar in Canaan, and took possession of the country in the name of the great Jehovah. Jacob bought a field in its neighborhood, which, by way of overplus, he gave to his son Joseph, who was buried there. After the conquest of Canaan it became a Levitical city of refuge in Ephraim, and a gathering-place of the tribes. Here Rehoboam gave the ten tribes occasion to revolt (I. Kings xii.). After the ruin of Samaria by Shalmaneser, Shechem became the capital of the Samaritans. At the present day it is also the seat of the small remnant of the Samaritans. It was called by the Romans Neopolis, from which the Arabs have made Napolose or Nabulus (John iv.).

Shiloh—A famous city of Ephraim, about ten miles south of Shechem, and twenty-four north of Jerusalem. Here Joshua assembled the people to make a second distribution of the land of promise; and here the tabernacle was set up when they were settled in the country. The ark and the tabernacle continued at Shiloh from 1444 B. C. to

1116 B. C., when it was taken by the Philistines under the administration of the high priest Eli.

Sidon—Now called Saida. It was a celebrated city of Phœnicia, on the Mediterranean Sea, twenty miles north of Tyre and as many south of Beyroot. It is one of the most ancient cities in the world, and is believed to have been founded by Zidon, the eldest son of Canaan. In the time of Homer (850 B. C.) the Zidonians were eminent for their trade and commerce, their wealth and prosperity, their skill in navigation, astronomy, architecture and for their manufactures of glass, etc. They had then a commodious harbor, now choked with sand and inaccessible to any but the smallest vessels. Upon the division of Canaan among the tribes of Joshua, Great Zidon fell to the lot of Asher; but that tribe never succeeded in obtaining possession. The Zidonians continued long under their own government and kings, though sometimes tributary to the kings of Tyre. They were subdued successively by the Babylonians, Egyptians and Romans, the latter of whom deprived them of their freedom. It is at present, like most of the other Turkish towns in Syria, dirty and full of ruins, though it still retains a little coasting trade, and has about five thousand inhabitants.

Sinai—A mountain, or mountain range, in Arabia Petræa in the peninsula formed by the two arms of the Red Sea, and rendered memorable as the spot where the law was given to Israel through Moses. The upper region of Sinai forms an irregular circle of thirty or forty miles in diameter, possessing numerous sources of water, a temperate climate and a soil capable of supporting animal and vegetable life: for which reason it is the refuge of all the Bedaweens when the low country is parched up. This, therefore, was the part of the peninsula best adapted to the residence of nearly a year, during which the Israelites were numbered, and received their laws from the Most

High. In the highest and central part of the region, seven thousand feet above the level of the sea, rises the sacred summit of Horeb or Sinai. The two names are used almost indiscriminately in the Bible. Scripture passages rather show that Horeb was the general name for the group, and Sinai the name of the sacred summit.

Symbol—A symbol is defined to be a visible sign with which a spiritual feeling, emotion or idea is connected. It was in this sense that the early Christians gave the name of symbols to all rites, ceremonies and outward forms which have a religious meaning; such, for instance, as the cross and other pictures and images, and even the sacraments and the sacramental elements. At a still earlier period the Egyptians communicated the knowledge of their esoteric philosophy in mystic symbols. "The first learning of the world," says Stukely, "consisted chiefly of symbols. The wisdom of the Chaldeans, Phœnicians, Egyptians, Jews, of all the ancients that is come to our hand, is symbolic." "Symbolical representations of things sacred," says Dr. Barlow, "were coeval with religion itself as a system of doctrine appealing to sense, and have accompanied its transmission to ourselves from the earliest known period of monumental history." Egyptian tombs and stiles exhibit religious symbols still in use among Christians. Similar forms, with corresponding meanings, though under different names, are found among the Indians, and are seen on the monuments of the Assyrians, the Etruscans and the Greeks. The Hebrews borrowed much of their early religious symbolism from the Egyptians, their later from the Babylonians, and through them this symbolic imagery, both verbal and objective, has descended to ourselves.

Syria—In Hebrew, Aram, a large district of Asia, lying, in the widest acceptation of the name, between the Mediterranean Sea on the west, the Taurus range on the north, the Tigris River on the east, and Arabia Deserta and

Palestine, or rather Judea, for the name Syria included also the northern part of Palestine, on the south. It was named after Aram, the son of Shem. Thus defined, it includes also Mesopotamia, which the Hebrews named Aram-Naha-raim (Aram of the two rivers—Tigris and Euphrates), or Padan-Aram (the plains of Aram or Syria), in distinction from the "mountains" of Aram. At the time of the Jewish exile Syria and Phœnicia were subject to the king of Babylon, and they afterwards were tributary to the Persian monarchs. Syria is now in the possession of the Turks. Its better portions have been thickly populated from a very early period, and travelers find traces of numerous cities wholly unknown to history.

Speculative Masonry—The lectures of the symbolic degrees instruct the neophyte in the difference between the Operative and the Speculative divisions of Masonry. They tell him that "we work in Speculative Masonry, but our ancient brethren wrought in both Operative and Speculative."

To the Freemason this Operative art has been symbolized in that intellectual deduction from it which has been correctly called Speculative Masonry. At one time each was an integral part of one undivided system. Operative Masonry was, in the inception of our history, and is in some measure even now, the skeleton upon which was strung the living muscles and tendons and nerves of the Speculative system. It was the block of marble, rude and unpolished it may have been, from which was sculptured the life-breathing statue.

Speculative Masonry (which is but another name for Freemasonry in its modern acceptation) may be briefly defined as the scientific application and the religious consecration of the rules and principles, the language, the implements and materials of Operative Masonry to the veneration of God, the purification of the heart and the inculcation of the dogmas of a religious philosophy.

Tadmor—A city founded by Solomon in the Desert of Syria, on the borders of the Arabian Desert towards the Euphrates. It was remote from human habitations on an oasis in the midst of a dreary wilderness; and it is probable that Solomon built it to facilitate his commerce with the East, as it afforded a supply of water, a thing of utmost importance in an Arabian desert. It was about 120 miles northeast of Damascus, more than half the distance to the Euphrates. The original name was preserved till the time of Alexander, who extended his conquest to this city, which then exchanged its name Tadmor for that of Palmyra, both signifying that it was a "City of Palms." It submitted to the Romans about the year 130, and continued in alliance with them during a period of 150 years. In the third century of our era, Odonathus, a native of Palmyra, established an independent Palmyrene kingdom, which was further extended, comprising the whole of Syria and parts of Mesopotamia, and brought to great prosperity by his widow, Queen Zenobia. But, when the queen refused to acknowledge the authority of Aurelian, the Roman emperor, he defeated her army, dissolved her empire, captured her capital and carried her away captive to Rome. When the Saracens triumphed in the East, they acquired possession of this city and restored its ancient name. It is still called Tadmor. Of the time of its first ruin there is no authentic record, but Masonic tradition ascribes it as having been destroyed by the Chaldeans and Babylonians about the year 600 B. C. It is thought, with some probability, that its last destruction occurred during the period in which it was occupied by the Saracens.

Tamarisk—The sacred tree of the Egyptian Mysteries, classically called the Erica. An evergreen tree, similar to the acacia.

Temple of Solomon—The foundations of this magnificent edifice were laid by Solomon in the year 1012 B. C. about 480 years after the exodus and the building of the tabernacle; and it was finished 1004 B. C., having occupied seven and a half years in the building. It retained its pristine splendor but thirty-three years, when it was plundered by Shishak, king of Egypt. After this period it underwent sundry profanations and pillages from other foreign rulers, and was at length utterly destroyed by Nebuchadnezzar, king of Babylon, 588 B. C., having stood 424 years. After lying in ruins for fifty-two years, the foundations of the second temple were laid by Zerubbabel and the Jews who had availed themselves of the privilege granted by Cyrus and returned to Jerusalem. After various hindrances, it was finished and dedicated in 515 B. C., twenty years after it was begun. In the year 163 B. C. this temple was plundered and profaned by Antiochus, who completely suspended the worship of Jehovah. After three years it was repaired and purified by Judus Maccabæus, who restored the divine worship and dedicated it anew.

King Herod, in the first year of his reign, 37 B. C., put to death all the Sanhedrim, except two, and after nearly twenty years of peace, through remorse of conscience, he resolved to rebuild and beautify the temple which at this time was in a state of decay. After two years in preparing the material for the work, the temple of Zerubbabel was pulled down in 17 B. C. and rebuilt in nine and a half years, yet a great number of laborers and artificers were still employed in carrying on the outbuildings all the time of our Saviour's abode on earth. The temple of Herod was considerably larger than that of Zerubbabel, as that of Zerubbabel was larger than Solomon's. All the Jewish writers praise this temple exceedingly for its beauty and the costliness of its workmanship. The whole structure above ground was completely demolished by Roman soldiers under Titus, A. D. 70.

Titan—The father of a race of giants called Titans, who contended with Saturn for the sovereignty of heaven, until Jupiter cast them by his thunderbolts into Tartarus, the place of punishment in Hades, or the lower world. The Titans, in their wars, are said to have piled mountains upon mountains to scale heaven, and they are taken as the types of lawlessness, gigantic size and enormous strength.

Typhon—The rival and opponent of his brother Osiris, whom he destroyed. He was considered the author of all the evil in the world. As Osiris was a type or symbol of the sun, Typhon was the symbol of winter, when the vigor, heat, and, as it were, life of the sun are destroyed, and of darkness as opposed to light.

Tyre—The celebrated emporium of Phœnicia, the seat of immense wealth and power, situated on the coast of the Mediterranean, within the limits of the tribe of Asher as assigned by Joshua, though never reduced to subjection. There was a close alliance between David and Hiram, king of Tyre, which was afterwards continued in the reign of Solomon; and it was from the assistance afforded by the Tyrians, both in artificers and materials, that the house of David, and afterwards the temple, were principally built. Tyre possessed the empire of the seas, and drew wealth and power from numerous colonies on the shores of the Mediterranean and Atlantic. The inhabitants of Tyre were filled with pride and luxury, and all the sins attendant on prosperity and immense wealth. It was the wealthiest and most magnificent of all Phœnician cities, and flourished for 3,000 years. Although taken and devastated successively by Shalmaneser, Nebuchadnezzar, Alexander the Great, the Saracens, the Crusaders and Salim I., it was always rebuilt. It stood twenty miles south of Sidon, and the locality it occupied was as strong in a military point of view as it was advantageous in commercial respects. One part of it was on the continent and the other on an adjacent island; the narrow sound which separated these two parts formed its harbor. After conquering the continental part of the city, Alexander the Great built a mole to the island by means of which he succeeded in conquering the insular part, too. This mole has in the course of time been transformed by alluvial deposits into a peninsula. But otherwise the remains which are left of this magnificent city are few and utterly insignificant. Its renowned manufactures are entirely dead, its commerce totally gone and a miserable village straggles along the site where once stood the richest storehouses and the most splendid palaces.

Ur—The country of Terah, and the birthplace of Abraham. It is usually called "Ur of the Chaldees," and is located, with strong probability, in the northwest part of Mesopotamia. The city of Orfah, to which the Jews make pilgrimages as the birthplace of Abraham, is a flourishing town of 30,000 inhabitants, seventy-eight miles southwest of Diarbekir. Some, however, place Ur in Lower Chaldea, at extensive ruins now called Warka.

Venus—The goddess of love, gracefulness, beauty and pleasure. Said to have sprung from the sea.

Wilderness of Paran—A large tract of desert country lying south of Palestine, and west of the valley El-Arabah, which runs from the Dead Sea to the Gulf of Akaba. It was in and near this desert region that the Israelites wandered thirty-eight years. It extended on the south to within three days' journey of Sinai, if not to Sinai itself. On the north it included the deserts of Kadesh and Zin. In the desert of Kadesh was situated the city of Kadesh-Barnea, which was said to lie in the "uttermost border of Edom," and was probably situated very near the great valley of El-Arabah, south of the Dead Sea. Kadesh was twice visited by the Israelites in their wanderings; once after they left Mount Sinai, and again thirty-eight years after. At the first visit the mission and return of the twelve spies took place, the rebellion of the people, and their presumptuous effort to enter Canaan by the pass Zephath, immediately north of Kadesh. At their second visit occurred the death of Miriam, the murmurings of the people for water, the miraculous supply, the sin of Aaron and Moses in smiting the rock, and the fruitless request for a passage through Edom (Num. xx. 1-22). In the desert of Zin, Hagar and Ishmael dwelt (Gen. xxi. 14-21).

Wilderness—See DESERT.

Wren, Sir Christopher—One of the most distinguished architects of England, born October 20, 1632; was the son of Dr. Wren, dean of Windsor and chaplain in ordinary to Charles I.; was distinguished in boyhood for mathematical and inventive genius; entered Wadham College, Oxford, at the age of fourteen. He built many fine buildings and churches, but his fame rests chiefly on St. Paul's Cathedral, which he built in 1675-1710. He was elected Grand Master of the Masons in 1685, an office he held until after the death of Queen Anne (1714), when he was removed by George I. He passed the few remaining years of his life in serene retirement. He was found dead in his chair after dinner on February 25, 1723, in the ninety-first year of his age, and was buried in the crypt of St. Paul's.

York—(Lat., *Eboracum*)—It is the capital of Yorkshire, at the confluence of the Ouse and Foss, and is one of the oldest and most interesting cities of England. It is surrounded with walls, and generally closely built with narrow streets and curious, old-fashioned houses. Its cathedral, built from the eleventh to the fourteenth century, is one of the finest specimens of Gothic architecture in the world. It is built in the form of a cross, 524 feet long, 250 feet broad across the transepts, with square, massive tower 225 feet high, rising over the crossing, and two elegant towers 196 feet high, flanking the western front. In the time of the Romans, York was the seat of the general government for the whole province of Britannia; and here Constantine the Great was proclaimed emperor. In the period of the Scots and the Danes it offered a fierce resistance to William

the Conqueror, who, after taking it, razed it to the ground.
It was only partially rebuilt, and suffered much by fire in
1137. This city is celebrated for its traditional connection
with Masonry in that kingdom. No topic in the history of
Freemasonry has so much engaged the attention of modern
Masonic scholars or given occasion to more discussion than
the alleged facts of the existence of Masonry in the tenth
century at the city of York, as the prominent point of the
calling of a congregation of the Craft there in 926, of the
organization of a General Assembly and the adoption of a
Constitution. "During the whole of the last and the greater
part of the present century the fraternity in general have
accepted all of these statements as genuine portions of
authentic history." (A. G. Mackey.)

Ziklag—A city of Judah and Simeon, on the borders
of the Philistines, who held it until the time of Saul, when
Achish, king of Gath, gave it to David. Hither many other
refugees from Judah resorted, and David was thus enabled
to aid Achish, and to chastise the Amalekites, who had
sacked Ziglag during his absence.

www.ingramcontent.com/pod-product-compliance
Lightning Source LLC
Chambersburg PA
CBHW060355030726
47497CB00003B/722